Shared Beliefs

Like love, like wrath, like hope, ambition, jealousy,

like every other instinctive eagerness and impulse,

it adds to life an enchantment which is not rationally or logically

deducible from anything else.

-William James

intro

The first thing we tend to ask about people's beliefs is: are they true? We want to

believe in 'the truth'. However, I see a much more addressable issue around belief arising out of

the way in which our beliefs affect the world, regardless of their veracity. Our beliefs are based

upon influences, the strongest of which appear to be based upon shared membership in a

group, whether that be a cultural subset, a national identity, a religious identity, or a complex

identity such as a participant in a scholarly discipline, for instance holding the identity of 'a

physicist'. Movements, such as political and revolutionary identities, as well as splinter groups

like self help movements, or cults, can also clearly serve as the nexus for an array of beliefs.

Geography has long had an effect upon group composition, and can sometimes be

reliably used to predict certain beliefs held by longtime residents. This tendency is on the

decline in many places however, contested by forces of conquest, conversion, reversion, and

other cultural influences seeking to de-homogenize an area. Naturally, there are shared beliefs

inherent within linguistic groups, because of the habit that language has of telling us what we

can say. Of course, outliers exist within all these types of groups, and there are many who hold

beliefs which are idiosyncratic. Still, influence persists while one is a member of a group, even within those groups which may seem innocuous, peripheral, or loose in their structure, such as those pursuing direct sales/multi level marketing, or participating in a team sport. The ethos of each of these groups provide a nexus of beliefs, and most people are part of many such groups simultaneously.

Beliefs are pervasive, but nebulous. To catch hold of some specific examples of influential belief groups, and examine them further, I have selected a cross section of case studies from around the world. No one subset, even that of religious beliefs, will be given a monopoly. The understanding that faith and affect are the driving force behind belief is widespread and ubiquitous. This book will examine the ways in which groups seek to use both this emotional sense of 'rightness' as it relates to shared concepts, as well as the way in which groups attempt to relate stated beliefs to logic and hard evidence, as conceived of through their particular lens of subjectivity. Religious beliefs will be touched upon, as well as online scams, conspiracy theories, beliefs around the court system, pseudo-archaeologies, sovereign citizens, as well as the effects of group beliefs on hard science, which is never as fully objective as it seems.

For the most part, this book is a simple inquiry into and cataloguing of narratives. It is also a synthesis of disparate ideas from across a variety of fields. Narratives proper are the subject, as they relate to the belief systems studied; they are generated and shared by the group, and they express the worldview and cosmology of the participants.

If enough people believe in something, does that make it true? Many gurus, life coaches, spiritual healers, and new age self help writers would have you accept that it does, and that your reality is created via your beliefs (and, presumably, the beliefs of those around you, although they don't usually go too deeply into it). Your beliefs about the universe are reflected in the conditions of your life, as you give and receive energy. Some of this thinking can be validated through the simple maxim that opportunities are accepted by those who are willing to accept them. It is obvious also that the degree to which you are engaged in your life will sometimes be reflected in your success. Still, it is clear that positive thinking, which resembles another emanation of the prosperity gospel, can actually be a negative thing in the sense that it shames those who are affected by institutional and societal barriers. The suggestion that white supremacy or intolerance of any form, once it has been reflected in calcified structures located in your area and embedded in the products of the 'dominant' culture, should be easily rejected through the use of a good attitude is beyond idealistic. It is harmful to make these statements, because although positive self-affirmation can help individuals to progress, it is not nearly all that is needed.

That said, it is evident that our beliefs have concrete effects. They affect our thoughts, and our actions, as we exist in the world. In 'The Human Condition' Hannah Arendt describes life as an action field, composed of multiplicities of intentions and interactions; the nature of this action field is such that the full consequences of our actions can never be predicted. She said, "The reason why we are never able to foretell with certainty the outcome and end of any action is simply that action has no end. The process of a single deed can quite literally endure throughout time until mankind itself has come to an end. That deeds possess such an enormous capacity for endurance, superior to every other man-made product, could be a matter of pride if men were able to bear its burden, the burden of irreversibility and unpredictability, from which the action process draws its very strength." (1958)

As I understand it, actions are based upon instinct, conditioning, emotion, and thought. Belief contributes to the functioning of three of those categories and is the driving force behind so much that we do together, whether it be, for instance, the shared rituals that give meaning to our lives, or conceptions around our life stages and what should take place in each. The cosmologies that we subscribe to are the result of a variety of interacting factors that determine the way in which we visualize and understand the universe and our place in it, so it is obvious that even the most ridiculous beliefs have concrete outcomes that can reify them (make them real).

Each culture, for instance, has different beliefs about even subjects as extreme as when it is permitted to kill another human being. Also, pain, often coded as bad because of its unpleasant nature, is also an absolutely necessary component in our lives, without which we would not be able to receive feedback on situations that might do damage to our physical bodies. To go farther, I also like to use the hypothetical example of a hurricane that took out an aquatic centre, among other structures. For humans, the event was coded negative in the extreme. For the shark, whose habitat was opened into the ocean, the event was likely coded positive and consisted of a release from captivity and greater capacity to function as an organism with that impediment gone. Though I cannot state that a group holds a 'wrong' belief, then, I can examine whether or not holding that belief seems to benefit participants, and also look into an accounting of the evidence around statements made by the group. This tells us whether or not, perhaps, the belief is compensating for a lack.

It is helpful to simply think of such relativism as stating the following: those things that matter to us, that enrich us, are important to us. William James, a 19th century pragmatic thinker who catalogued religious experiences, wrote about this in his book, On A Certain Blindness in Human Beings (1900). He said, "Our judgments concerning the worth of things, big or little, depend on the feelings the things arouse in us. Where we judge a thing to be precious in consequence of the idea we frame of it, this is only because the idea is itself associated already with a feeling. If we were radically feelingless, and if ideas were the only things our mind could entertain, we should lose all our likes and dislikes at a stroke, and be unable to point to any one situation or experience in life more valuable or significant than any other. Now the blindness in human beings, of which this discourse will treat, is the blindness with which we all are afflicted in regard to the feelings of creatures and people different from ourselves... Hence the stupidity and injustice of our opinions, so far as they deal with the significance of alien lives. Hence the falsity of our judgments, so far as they presume to decide in an absolute way on the value of other persons' conditions or ideals."

Ultimately, the fact that we are all human leaves much room to share a variety of ideals with one another. Trying to place the ideals of one culture upon another, however, has been soundly proven wrong by colonial outcomes still reverberating in North America, where I write, and elsewhere. I try to allow cosmologies to function as ethical concept-clusters, and to study them without enforcing the culture of myself, the scholar, upon them. Still, we are all in an unpredictable action field, and so we know that there is a constant struggle between ideologies and cosmologies here on Earth. I see a well meaning impetus, for instance, to bring ideas that work in one part of the world to another, but it is important to note that a positive result somewhere has never equated to a positive result everywhere.

I see war as wrong. But, when small raids and inter-tribal warfare serves as a redistribution mechanism for camels, for instance, and the entire economy of an area relies on that mechanism, notions of 'harm' and 'good' must be seen in light of this schema. (Sweet 1969) Is it war that is wrong, or is it nationalism and technology that has made warfare, as I know it, too large-scale and untenable for the group I belong to? I will choose not to go into the various justifications, across cultures, used to view war as righteous in certain circumstances, dictated by variant shared ideals seen as worth dying for.

Attempting to see issues in terms of multiple perspectives has led me into the use of Kidder's 4 Paradigms (1997), an ethical analysis tool that helps us to understand beliefs based on the priorities of those who hold them. This system, developed in the west, still reflects Eurocentric ways of thinking. However, it can provide insight when juxtaposed upon those who oppose one another on the basis of belief-- a common phenomenon. The paradigms are: justice vs. mercy, long term vs. short term, loyalty vs. honesty, and individual vs. community. I have found that these categories break down when you begin to deal with societies without as much Western influence, such as China, which has another set of ethical clusters that are just as interesting and paradoxical. Nonetheless, these paradigms might be helpful to you as we explore the case studies, and even perhaps during your next difference of opinion with someone you know.

We may yet develop a comprehensive set of shared ethics that transcends our differences as humans, and this is something I am not willing to rule out. It would be presumptuous to assume that what I see as right or wrong at this time in history will be tapped as universally applicable by this future, thus erasing so many valid ways of life by its existence. Imagining universality and homogeneity constitutes flirting with genocide. Where the paradigms do not apply, ethical concept clusters should be sought out and 'translated', thus revealing which ideals are problematic or in conflict with one another within the context of the group being studied.

This book will not classify beliefs as 'right' or 'wrong', therefore. Occasionally factuality in terms of the 'correct' or 'incorrect' nature of certain statements will be examined, in the sense of examining whether or not the group puts stock in factual, empirical evidence in order to reinforce shared beliefs, or whether such evidence is unimportant within the belief system. Such evidence may be discussed when evaluating the effect of the shared belief on participants on others. I am very interested in the area where faith interacts with reason, and is presented as logical or reasonable.

It is my hope that these case studies are fascinating and accessible to the layman, while also holding the potential to direct academic study towards a richer exploration of the phenomena touched upon here. What we believe says so much about us-- ultimately, our beliefs reveal that which we desire to be true above all else. That simple sentence serves as my central thesis, and when applied to each case study, longing unfolds itself and lets us know what it is that group participants truly desire. There are certain things we NEED to be true, in order to give us a feeling of fitness and rightness, so that we can make sense of where we are. Beliefs let us know what our needs are. Members of the groups from the case studies are persons with whom you might share a milieu. Examining what they need, and the concrete effects of the resultant needs, is an enriching process.

It is important to note that beliefs are bought and sold, and can be generated by beings or entities who may or may not subscribe to them. The effects of these generated shared beliefs are, therefore, sometimes not correlated with the values that produced attachment among group members influenced by the generated ideology, and the effects can ultimately betray the group at large in favour of the 'leaders'. The attitudinal beliefs inculcated by multi level marketing corporations in their participants, for instance, benefit the companies, at the expense of the participant in the vast majority of cases, despite sounding and seeming positive and easy to identify with. One percent of individuals at the top will also profit.

The company materials may teach, "The only way to lose is to quit! Believe in yourself and there is no stopping you!" thus causing the participant to hang on and continue spending their money attempting to succeed as a consultant, while ignoring the fact that logically we should invest only in something that produces revenue. Often, the emotional benefit of being within a group is used to blind participants to the fact that failure rate in the multi level marketing industry is over 99%. (Vesoulis 2020) As a teenager, I was used by a corporation in this way, and persuaded to become a customer, in the guise of an employee. These corporations trade in belief, as well as the feeling that there 'should' be an escape from conventional working life, that it would be 'right' to avoid the stress of having a boss and being exploited as a wage worker, but the end result is financial devastation.

It goes without saying that this is a book influenced by philosophy. In the Western tradition, there is a tendency to separate philosophy from action, and to bring it into the realm of absolutes or the throes of the hypothetical. I believe that philosophy is most needed at the level of understanding that takes place in the course of our everyday lives, in the encounters we have and the choices we make. The groups listed here are operating in the here and now, offering beliefs to you and hoping that they will hold appeal. Many of these groups I've used in my case studies aim to serve or to analyze you, to have influence over you, or relation with you. Understanding them and what they reveal of being human may help you to engage with situations you come across while existing in the world with greater clarity. All beliefs create structures of power around themselves.

Go forth with this caveat:

"I know well enough that that every word I utter

carries with it something of myself...

with its particular history and its own particular world.

Even when I deal with empirical data,

I am necessarily speaking about myself." (Jung 1933)

1. Alternative History in Mormonism

Joseph Smith was a man, born in Vermont, who lived during the time of the Great Awakening. Largely uneducated, he nonetheless became the charismatic leader of a new religion. He purportedly received a text from an angel, engraved into gold plates, bearing a message in an enigmatic language that Joseph referred to as Reformed Egyptian. (McDannell 2017) He called himself a translator, bringing God's latest testament into the vernacular, but he did not do so textually, but rather, "with his seer stone, gazing into the bottom of a hat all those hours and days as he sat concealed behind the blanket veil and gave dictation." (Price 2003) This divinatory practice served to answer a question, so crucial in that sectarian time of comparative religious freedom on the frontier: what did God want from present day Christians? Smith, a man of visions, was poised to answer this question.

Most of us in North America are aware of Mormonism, considered by some to be a world religion. It is a combination of Christianity with the ideal of American exceptionalism, and it is also disavowed by mainline Christian denominations, despite sharing overlapping holy texts. "In April 2011, The Church of Jesus Christ of Latter-day Saints announced that it had distributed the 150 millionth copy of the Book of Mormon... By the year 2000, the Church was printing one copy every seven seconds. Translated into eighty-two languages, the book is considered by Latter-day Saints to be 'another testament of Jesus Christ.'" (McDannell 2017) Clearly, the Book of Mormon and the group of people who believe in it have been influential.

The idea of modern prophets was key to the period in America when Smith lived, and it was a common desire to re-evoke a truly Biblical way of life. Polygamy, for which Mormons were criticized by many contemporary religious groups, is an example of one revival of Biblical custom, meant to reflect the desire to live in a way sanctioned directly by God. Of course, it was also an idea amenable to and originated by men, who may have simply desired to have more than one wife. Interestingly, Smith's wife Emma was resistant to it.

I thought of Mormonism as just another American denominative splinter group, until I realized that it also constitutes an alternative history. In its way, the Christian Bible could also be called an alternative history, since among many anomalies, textual sources from other cultures around the time of the Old Testament indicate that the Hebrews were not nearly as sumptuous or important as they portrayed themselves to be (Merneptah Stele, Lachish Reliefs, etc). Yet, there are archaeological records indicating their existence in the region of Canaan, regardless of narrative differences, and so instead the Old Testament sits alongside other late Bronze Age cultural products and bespeaks its own time.

The Book of Mormon is notably different in nature, published in 1830 but proposing to tell of events occurring on the continent two thousand years earlier. (McDannell 2017) The Book of Mormon is a revealed document, claimed to be transmitted directly from the Angel Moroni, who lived in North America in those ancient times, and dictated by Smith to his followers, who wrote it down for him.

Narratives around the authorship of the Book of Mormon are varied, even within the religion. "Did Joseph Smith write the Book of Mormon? To this over-familiar question the orthodox Latter-day Saint answer is a resounding 'No' because the official belief is that a series of men with quasi-biblical names wrote the book over many centuries. For some critics of Mormonism the answer is an equally emphatic No, but for a different reason. Such critics have charged that the Book of Mormon was plagiarized from Solomon Spaudling's lost novel of Israelites in ancient America, 'Manuscript Found.' A third group, liberal Mormons and fellow travelers, tend to recognize Joseph Smith as the author of the book, inspired though he may perhaps have been by earlier works such as Ethan Smith's View of the Hebrews." (Price 2003)

The story that Smith dictated was related to a common conspiracy theory of the time, which posited that the British, as a people, were actually the descendants of the Lost Tribes of Israel. (Price 2003) The term Lost Tribes is used to refer to ten of the original twelve Biblical tribes who were said to have been scattered by Neo-Assyrian conquest, their locations unknown to recorded history. As indicated above, The Book of Mormon also appeared to incorporate other existing ideas from a book published a few years earlier in 1823, Views of the Hebrews, by Ethan Smith. Like Views of the Hebrews, the Book of Mormon discussed the movement of the Lost Tribes of Israel into the Americas, and espoused the idea that the indigenous peoples were descended from them and the land consecrated by their presence.

Smith's suggestion that massive warring groups described in the Book of Mormon filled the Americas, where they were in direct anachronistic contact with Jesus, does not agree with archaeology or genetic analysis in the main. However, it could be suggested that it agreed with some of the loose scholarship produced in Smith's own era, including the idea that the presence of Israel's Lost Tribes could consecrate an area as God's new favourite. The scholarly line in archaeology in Smith's time also indicated a lost civilization in America, known as the Mound

Builders. This civilization appears to have been largely invented by colonizers reacting in surprise to the massive earthworks scattered around the Great Lakes and the Mississippi river valley, which they assumed were too sophisticated to be built by earlier generations of the indigenous people in the area, who had, of course, actually built them. (Frey 1879) Naturally, it appears as if Smith's answer to this conundrum was in line with popular thought: spectacular achievements must be connected with Judeo-Christian traditions and genetics in order to account for their impressive nature.

Mormon apologetics (this term refers to documents written to defend and promote a specific religion) is full of such 'rationalism', because the religion caught on in an era when scientific inquiry was itself making strides. Smith himself interacted with historical documents, and claimed to be able to read hieroglyphics, inaccurately interpreting a fragment of the Book of the Dead he had purchased as a narrative related to Moses. The gold plates themselves appear to be a reference to the type of discovery reported to be happening at the time as the field of archaeology started to expand, were said to have been seen by eight witnesses, and were posited as factual and real, dug up by Smith at the direction of the aforementioned Angel Moroni.

The witnesses, however, despite their labelling as such, actually affirmed that they had seen the plates in a vision. Still, it is evident that credibility is sought through the use of the term, 'witness' as well as the term 'translate'. A preoccupation with history is evident in Mormonism. "The Book of Mormon is not solely an ethical guideline; it is a report from the past. For orthodox Mormons, Joseph Smith translated the Book of Mormon from real gold plates, and the text documented the complicated history of real ancient peoples. Throughout his life, Joseph Smith rejected the Protestant notion that the extraordinary experiences of Jesus and the apostles were trapped in the past. As a prophet, he unlocked the world of the supernatural—making the divine-human interaction simultaneously more literal and more personal than was customary in Protestant America. Over the centuries, as influential groups of Americans became more rational and more willing to accept layered interpretations of the Bible, Mormons continued to call potential believers to ask: is the Book of Mormon true or is it false?" (McDannell 2017)

Smith documented his work with the supposed Reformed Egyptian language, writing out some of the characters of the language and claiming that it arose out of hieroglyphic writing, positioning it as a kind of alternative sister language to the actual progression of hieratic, demotic, and coptic writing systems in Egypt. He documented his translation of the Book of the Dead fragment, as a scholar would, but his reading of it as the story of Moses was not in agreement with contemporary translations of hieroglyphics.

It is obvious that Smith had an inquiring, but unschooled mind, and some claim that his lack of education is proof of divine inspiration for the Book of Mormon, because he did not have the necessary knowledge or experience to consciously write in chiasmus, for instance. Though the concept of chiasmus, a type of poetic device common in the Bible and said to have originated in ancient Hebrew, was not named in his time, Joseph Smith evidently had plenty of experience with the King James Version, its poetics, and its metre. (Welch 1969) He perhaps lacked the experience to know that a translated document would not reproduce the English version of the Bible so faithfully, as the Book of Mormon seems to contain several sections that seem to be lifted directly from it. Still, apologists claim that this concordance is due to God's perfection, which cannot be explicitly disproved.

Mormonism mainly tries to use science in two ways. First, Mormons say that the Book of Mormon is backed up by archaeological, and other, evidence, thus indicating that veracity is important and bringing the concept of 'proof' into the arena of faith. Second, Mormons envision the Book of Mormon, as a perfect document, actually assisting science by directing and anticipating future discoveries, which are obviously in existence somewhere because the book came as a perfect document from God, thus attempting to bring articles of faith into science. Brigham Young University, for instance, continues even now to search within academic disciplines like linguistics and archaeology for proof that demonstrates the events in the Book of Mormon as factually real. In a paper published under its auspices, Clark wrote in 2005, "An over- riding question in Book of Mormon scholarship is: did Joseph Smith write or translate the book? Any fair understanding of Joseph Smith must derive from a plausible explanation of the Book of Mormon, and both science and reason can and should be involved in the evaluation."

I'm going to go further into Clark's paper, titled Archaeological Trends and Book of Mormon Origins, because it is a perfectly typical example of Mormon scholarship. It seeks to prove that, of course, the text was translated by Smith rather than written by him, and so the paper intends to demonstrate that Smith did not have a deep understanding of that which he had dictated. Clark says, "Thanks in large part to his critics, it is becoming clear that Joseph Smith did not fully understand the geography, scope, historical scale, literary form, or cultural content of the book. For example, early Mormons believed Book of Mormon lands stretched throughout all of North and South America, a presumption clearly at odds with the book itself.

The book speaks specifically only of a limited land about the size of Pennsylvania. In 1842, after reading about ancient cities in Central America, Joseph speculated that Book of Mormon lands were located there. I derive two lessons from his speculation: First, Joseph did not know exactly where Book of Mormon lands were; second, he considered their location an important question addressable through scholarship. The book makes hundreds of claims about ancient peoples in the Americas. It has always been clear to people on both sides of the controversy that antiquities could be, and should be, used to corroborate or destroy the books pedigree." (2005)

In order to avoid confronting issues like lack of linguistic connection between indigenous languages and Hebrew, lack of DNA evidence connecting indigenous people in America with Canaanites, lack of grave goods with any connection to Hebraic traditions, lack of documented animal remains for species named in the Book of Mormon as residing in the Americas, and other thorny questions, Clark focuses exclusively upon geography and population. "The book describes a narrow, hour-glass-shaped territory several hundred miles long that is sandwiched between eastern and western seas. John Sorenson has demonstrated that southern Mexico and northern Central America fit remarkably well the book's geography in overall size, configuration, and location of physical features. Book of Mormon geography fits a corner of the Americas Joseph did not know. Therefore, the book's geography could not have derived from his personal experience. It follows that he dictated a book with complexities beyond his own comprehension." (2005)

I would argue that if you are willing to span whole continents in order to place a described geography somewhere, you may be taking a preconceived notion and finding a location for it, and nothing has been demonstrated if so. This is the mapping of belief, and we can see in the article that there is a literal map drawn based on the geographic description in the book that makes the literary place visual and accompanies Clark's words. The map is shaped like an hourglass with seas on both sides, and bears place names like, 'Land of Zarahemla' and 'narrow strip of wilderness'. No place names, not even the names of the seas, indicate any relationship with established geography. Based on a glance at an actual map of Mexico, we are left to assume that the seas are the Pacific and the Gulf of Mexico and that the hourglass consists of Veracruz and Oaxaca on one side and Tabasco and Chiapas on the other.

Clark then embarks on a process of attempting to demonstrate that the Jaredites, an ancient group from the Book of Mormon, were actually the Olmec, and that the Nephites, another group named in the book, were actually the Maya. Proof is scanty, consisting of basically identifying the group that exists in the archaeological record in the right place at the right time, and deciding that it corresponds with the group living at that time period in the Book of Mormon narrative. We also get this: "As the consummate recordkeepers in Mesoamerica, the Maya erected numerous stone monuments in their cities that recorded the time elapsed since 3114 BC, their year zero. Maya calculations were based on counting by twenties instead of our practice of counting by tens. The major cycle of Maya time was a four-hundred-year period called a baktun. The Book of Mormon records several references to a significant four-hundred-year prophecy, consistent with this idiosyncratic Mesoamerican calendar practice." (Clark 2005) These practices are conflated together in order to demonstrate the remote possibility, already roundly contradicted by genetic evidence, that these are the same peoples.

It is the habit of Mormon faith, and faith in general, to manifest a new way of looking. McDannell, a scholar focused on Mormonism, reports that this type of investigation and witnessing is central to Mormonism. She studies the phenomenon of Mormons making trips to Mexico to view ruins, and posits that this type of tourism allows for a deeper belief that is based on seeing, saying that, "to maintain a conviction in a truth one must not simply 'believe it.' Belief must be cultivated through bodily acts and through spiritual experiences." (2017)

McDannell discusses the way in which American Mormons proceed on guided tours, led by Mexican Mormons who draw parallels between the physical nature of the ruins and their powerful presence, and the spiritual narratives of the Book of Mormon, without ever becoming overly explicit. Relations are suggested and evoked, allowing for an alternative explanation for the sites, which are already demonstrably related to specifically Mayan culture by archaeology, in the light of shared Mormon faith. "Well aware of the discrepancies between archaeological dating and Book of Mormon events, the guides discuss the ruins and the people who made the ruins in terms of their ability to carry the fragmentary remains of an ancient truth." (2017) This vague allusiveness allows for Mormon visitors to feel relation to the sites on an emotional and spiritual level.

What desires are revealed here? First, the desire for communication with God to be continuous. In the 1800s, Protestantism has succeeded in many places at bringing the Bible into the local vernacular. Interpretation of it was varied and meant to be personally experienced, including, among the Quakers for instance, the holding of personal revelation on par with the Bible. For many people, this probably created an unbearable ambiguity because it became difficult to have an absolute answer to the matter of what God wanted from his creatures. Hand in hand with that was a sensation of closeness with God, granted by the encouragement of reading the Bible for oneself. The idea of a personal relationship with a divine being was ripe during the Great Awakening, encouraging in its wake such a variety of sects that Smith himself stated that there were too many, and that he sensed that it was an impossibility for all to be right or acceptable, before he had his first vision. (Price 2003)

Authority was needed, and sought through direct communication with God, as well as, in a lesser way, through science. There is, in other words, an obsession with factuality within a contested field of Christian sects that bespeaks how literally the difference between salvation and doom lay in man's ability to interpret what God wants. During times when existent knowledge is not enough to make an informed choice, new knowledge tends to be gained by divinatory means. The Book of Mormon clears up, for its followers, a variety of theological issues widespread among Christians, including whether or not children who die without baptism will be saved, whether or not the death of Jesus on the cross equalled eternal salvation for all, or only some, whether resurrection will be physical, or only spiritual, whether the fall of man was always part of God's divine plan, whether faith alone or good works are required in order to be redeemed.

These are among the very questions that had caused branches of Christianity to separate from one another, so it's easy to see why people would be pleased to see them answered by revelation (all of these examples were taken directly from the central Church of Jesus Christ website at churchofjesuschrist.org). There is an impetus toward universalizing in Mormonism, and a desire to affirm free will which is appropriate to its time, and can be located as a kind of resistance to the influence of movements like Calvinism, with its idea that only the elect have the capacity for salvation.

Then, there is geography. Why must America be special? The myth of American exceptionalism, so important to so many, is bolstered effectively by having Gods chosen people brought there. A place, with inhabitants and history of its own, is given a new history in order to emphasize its destiny. To quote from the Book of Mormon directly, "whatsoever nation shall possess [the promised land of the Book of Mormon peoples] shall be free from bondage, and from captivity, and from all nations under heaven, if they will but serve the God of the land, who is Jesus Christ." (Ether 2:12.) Alternative history is often used to express desires that are current at the time that they originate, and are largely unrelated to values or events occurring during the time period they purport to cover. In this way they provide authority for the domination of others, whether physical or representative, by the culture making use of the narrative, and overwriting the history of subjugated peoples in the process.

The Protocols of the Elders of Zion, a forgery, expressed anti-Semitic desire and was simultaneously a means of oppression against Jewish people as its message of conspiracy spread and became popular. Fomenko's New Chronology is similar, positing as it does a worldwide conspiracy to erase Russia's central role in history, not coincidentally written just after the events of WWII, presumably to justify Communist Russia's expansion into an empire. (Larouelle 2012) It makes a lot of logical sense that America would inherit the concept of manifest destiny from Britain, and along with it, the supposition of a relation to the Lost Tribes. The provision of a history, during a time when indigenous perspectives on history were unacceptable to linear Western minds, was required in Smith's mind in order to make sense of the landscape and European presence in it. A strong desire for relation is manifest, a desire to feel right and 'in place' in the land that settlers had claimed as their own.

When Mormons are approaching converts, these associations are what actually composes the specific dream that they are offering. As they offer it to people in the global south, it is evident that reification around the idea of America and what it has to offer is taking place alongside digested spiritual content. A re-writing of indigenous past in the light of Judeo-Christian heritage turns a plurality of cultures present in the Americas into homogeneous agreement, revealing a desire to have always owned all of this land, and the assumed superiority of Western rationalism.

Interestingly, when it comes to belief in practice, many Mormon respondents on the question and answer website, Quora, stated that when they attempted to use logic to question elements of the official history, they were instructed that the only crucial element of belief was the feeling of 'burning in the breast.' All logic and consistency is in practice outweighed by this sense of rightness that comes directly from God. Here we can see that rational apologetics is what faith has used to clothe itself, revealing an inner core of devout trust. All of the scholarship appears to give the impression of inquiring, while upon closer inspection it seems to proceed out of sureness, never constituting an actual investigation.

A similar, but more recent overwriting of history informed by nationalism that you could choose to investigate and engage with in the world is the removal and destruction of artifacts associated with Armenia by Azerbaijan. In the next section, we will examine another contemporary rewriting of the geographic and historic landscape, a key difference being that this next narrative of greatness and mysticism was set in motion by residents of a recently

subjugated nation.

2. Alternative Archaeology in Bosnia

The Bosnian pyramid complex is supposedly the largest and oldest in the world, dated by Semir Osmanagic to over 34,000 years ago. The complex is positioned to line up with stellar objects, and it is perfectly positioned along a significant global parallel and corresponds with 'cardinal points'. Tests by scientific teams from around the world have apparently confirmed a variety of site-specific phenomena, including high concentrations of healing ions. The site is also significant to the world's scientific community, because it sits outside of the mainstream and threatens established research and tenure-- at least according to Osmanagic.

His findings have been roundly rejected by all important institutions, including a direct rebuttal from the European Association of Archaeologists. To quote that body in referring to his excavation, "It is a waste of scarce resources that would be much better used in protecting the genuine archaeological heritage and is diverting attention from the pressing problems that are affecting professional archaeologists in Bosnia-Herzegovina on a daily basis." In fact, atop the 'Pyramid of the Sun' there is a documented medieval era ruin, the condition of which archaeologists have become concerned about due to Osmanagic's amateur excavations in the area. (Harris 2006, Ramadanovic 2008)

But, Semir has found some believers, whose labour he uses to excavate at what he calls, "the largest active archaeological site in the world." He has also built a tourism industry around the town of Visoko, catered to by a community of volunteers from around the world. Also, there is a gift shop where a representative of Osmanagic sells pyramid water and handicrafts. A lengthy tour in English by a kind young woman of an underground tunnel beneath the 'complex' can be seen on Youtube (and you can watch it via a link in the works cited list for this chapter). The woman uses a variety of infographics to bolster her points, as she informs visitors that the tunnels were dug, and then filled in, by an unknown ancient group. She instructs the tourists to place their hands on a monolithic rock that she indicates as having healing, meditative energies. The water in the tunnels is claimed to be the healthiest water on Earth, and the air in the tunnels, the purest.

She says, "this is the safest place on earth. There are no poisonous gases, no negative energy, nothing....This will be our first stop. This is the first artifact that we found here. It's called egg shaped monolith. As we know, egg represents birth, life, so we assume that is the reason why they put it at the beginning. We ask ourselves, why is it positioned in this right position? We scanned this surface, and we found out something interesting. As we may know, underground waters represent something negative. So, we decided that...one of the walls...the groundwater flows from that direction, goes right underneath it, and goes that way. This egg shaped monolith is made out of a case, and a lid. Inside, we have quartz crystal....we ask ourselves again, why is it there? When water flows, it creates a negative energy, it, lifted, hits the quartz crystal and creates a positive electromagnetic field here..." (Her English is very good, and she trails off only occasionally when she is looking for a word.)

The Archaeological Park Foundation, based out of Visoko and led by Osmanagic, unsurprisingly does not involve the labour of professionals from that field. Rather, work at the pyramid complex and attendant labyrinth of underground tunnels is fuelled by the democratization of science, and the incorporation within scientific-sounding discourse of faith based subjective ideas. For the price of your time toward the excavation, Osmanagic provides you with the opportunity to get your hands dirty on a dig, regardless of your skill level. The view he espouses in multiple of his videos is that scientific education in a formal sense is indoctrination that prevents the holder from interacting meaningfully and honestly with historical data, and this view appeals to the participants, who enter the complex as skeptics of the establishment.

On the Foundation's website, you can experience such things as, 'Scalar energy Zoom call: Arcturus Ra & Prof Sam Osmanagich' (this is a variant spelling of his last name, the Bosnian language uses the Cyrillic alphabet, so variant spellings into English are common) and 'Spectacular Results of Dating in Ravne 3 Tunnels'. The dating of 15-20,000 years is indeed spectacular, but tested material was taken from stalagmites that formed in a cave encountered in the tunnels below the complex, and there is no evidence that the 'man-made drywalls' cited there as present below the stalagmites and therefore inferred to be older, are man made at all. The use of words like 'concrete' and 'drywall' to refer to the strata found onsite is especially notable -- by agreeing to use this vernacular at all, people discussing the finds have already unwittingly committed to Osmanagic's frame of reference.

A community of seekers has been created around the 'pyramid complex', which has been determined by geologists to be naturally occurring hills. (Traynor 2006) A new type of looking has been established onsite, whereby that which is desired can be noted in the landscape itself, if one is willing to believe. Comments on the various Archaeological Park video productions are telling. Adib Khan comments on Youtube, in response to the video Dr.Sam Osmanagich - My Story, "Exactly the thing I was looking for. Civilized human [sic] couldn't be only 6 thousand or some years old. The way you say that its not about evolution, its about cycles, I loved that. Its really shameful how narrow minded and egoistic modern historians are. We need to rewrite history ASAP. Keep up your good work sir and congratulations for your amazing discovery. Hope you will complete your excavation soon and open eyes of the mainstream archeologists [sic] and historians. Want to see more of your interviews."

This particular type of 'looking', situated by its proponents in the domain of scientific observation, is typified for me in a Youtube video by a user associated with the project. It is as if the act of looking, seeing what one longs for, and being carried away by the depth of what one sees, constitutes a legitimate means of generating fact. The Youtube user is Travis Bryant and the title of the video is *Bosnian Pyramid of the Sun (Piramida Sunca) obvious concrete blocks vid 1 (Visoko, Bosnia) 6-29-13.* It has received over 14,000 views. You can find this video and others that I have mentioned in the works cited for this chapter.

The camera plays over a variety of stones on the ground as Bryant states, "Concrete blocks, upwards of 100 tons...Clear concrete conglomerate material...Who doesn't believe this is, you know, a manmade structure?...I am so over that...I mean, come on son, concrete conglomerate, five, five to twelve times stronger than any concrete we can make today...made of bedrocks, and sand, and heated tremendously to make this concrete." He goes on to discuss the fact that modern concrete apparently absorbs more water than does this material, leading to the suggestion that the ancients were extremely effective builders. Superficially, the rocks do resemble concrete, and for Bryant, such a resemblance, along with influence from Osmanagic, decides the issue in favour of the presence of super-ancient and perfect building blocks.

The Bosnian government's endorsement of the project, and the idea of 'looking' as paramount in science, is summed up and rebutted succinctly by Heinrich (2007) : "Bosnian Prime Minister Nedzad Brankovic is quoted as asking, 'Why don't we recognize something that is visible to the naked eye?' An answer to his question is that Semir Osmanagic and his colleagues have so far failed to publish, in a peer-reviewed journal, a credible case that the ruins of a monument constructing 'supercivilization' are anything other than a haphazard collection of jointed bedrock, Leisegang banding, sole marks, concretions, and other geologic features mixed in with some unrelated medieval, Roman, and other artifacts and ruins."

For me, this will to see that which is not actually verified as present appears to be a trauma response. Not only do people feel excluded from the sciences, perceiving those who confer knowledge as gatekeepers unfriendly to open-minded exploration, but also and most importantly the region itself was war-torn in the 1990s by the Bosnian war and acts of genocide against the Bosniak minority in what was then Yugoslavia. Osmanagic assuages both of these issues by revitalizing the area financially, through the attraction of new age oriented tourists and volunteers with spending money, and emotionally, through the provision of a narrative wherein the oldest and most impressive pyramidal structures in the world MUST be located there. Visoko appears as a place of importance in the actual archaeological record, through the established discovery of medieval settlement, but this in itself was not enough to captivate those who required that the area be one of primary importance on the world stage.

True redemption needed more than what was self-evident: Visoko, and by association, Bosnia, had to transcend in a very definite way. This place was to become the lynchpin of a transformation in the way Bosnians, and humans, saw themselves and their history: rejection of the established archaeological and historical facts, rejection of the scientific establishment itself, and rejection of the accomplishments of other, disparate cultures in favour of a truly stunning narrative. It is not surprising that the project is condoned by the Bosnian government. The villagers benefit monetarily from the project through increased tourism revenue, including housing and feeding the large number of volunteers and visitors who cycle through.

Those who arrive to work on the project, bearing money and donating their time, see it as a revitalization of open-minded discourse in which the fantastic can, and should be, true. The desire to see opportunities for new and startling insights as endless is very positive for participants, who often speak of the benefits of the community they have joined. The community reinforces participant beliefs by providing shared affirmation of such concepts as miraculous healing and advanced technology powered by nature, the secrets of which can be found through the study of ancient history. The ancient people who possessed such technology might symbolize a new way forward for believers, during this time when human development has made the Earth inhospitable and affected biodiversity. The volunteers want to be healed through their participation, and they can be compared to pilgrims because their presence is a physical manifestation of their belief. Visoko is their holy place.

For me, the volunteers fulfill the role of both witnesses and terraformers, stuck in a cycle of altering the landscape and looking at that altered landscape in relation to an ancient, and supposedly better, way of being. Their labour both reveals and creates the formations found onsite, as the denuding of dirt and vegetation expose and reinforce the concrete blocks they 'see', creating a new Bosnia in the process. The two groups, who both stand to benefit from their beliefs in very different ways, have reached a sort of symbiosis. Most of the visitors and volunteers don't seem to feel a connection with Bosnian nationalism, and most of the villagers don't seem to be involved with broader the new age movement, or invested in the inner need to reject science as calcified and dictatorial. Rather, they connect the idea of a bright future with the 'fact' that the area was once so significant.

The scientific establishment, in dealing with the fact that so many people have been exposed to the pyramid and its mythic connotations, expresses itself on the matter in a variety of papers. Here is a quote from one by Heinrich in 2007: "no matter how obviously natural the various features that comprise pseudo-archaeological sites are to conventional geologists and archaeologists, dismissing them as 'pseudoscience' is not enough. Instead, we need to explain to the public using empirical data and logical arguments published in either popular articles, field guidebooks, Web pages, or other media how natural features are either being misidentified or misrepresented as cultural artifacts. The wide interest generated by Bosnian 'pyramids,' the 'Phoenician Furnace and Fortress' of Oklahoma, and other pseudo-archaeological sites offers an opportunity to educate a curious public about the origin and significance of the geologic features such as systematic jointing, Leisegang banding, ripple marks, sole marks, and concretions that comprise them."

I strongly disagree with this proposed solution. I don't detect that the need that the volunteers have for a narrative emphasizing human accomplishment, and their additional perceived need for freer thought within a discipline, regardless its realism, can be addressed by discussion of geologic features, because this is a process in which the 'curious public' cannot participate adequately. I also do not suppose that scientific fact will bear out the unique cultural productions of one region in Bosnia being situated above all the world's other cultural productions, especially since the hills in question do not satisfy the criteria necessary to fulfill being 'man-made'. I would argue that the temporary advantage of believing that Visoko is the centre of an ancient civilization has proven to be effective for regional revitalization. It remains to be seen whether or not a project with genuine findings would serve as effectively as a collective myth to bolster a group of people who have suffered deeply. Certainly misinformation is damaging because it prevents people from engaging on an informed level.

I would also suggest that the Bosnian government is taking advantage of the project because it serves as a form of symbolic appeasement for their population. Symbolic appeasement refers to the fact that the population can receive comfort from any number of actions on the government's behalf, some of which are connected directly to resources, and therefore costly, and others, like a public acknowledgement, that do not cost the government much time or money. (Edelman 1985) Though some token government funds have found their way to the Archaeological Park, such funds pale in comparison with what it would really cost to revitalize industry and community in the Visoko area through government initiative. It is likely that symbolic appeasement through myth-making will always hold a great deal of appeal at the governmental level worldwide, absolving as it does some of the need for resource-based action. For all these reasons, the Bosnian government is actually another beneficiary of the project.

For now, let's focus on the volunteers, because I would suggest that their experience in achieving that which they desire has been more ambivalent. After all, the volunteers aimed to engage in science, and make contributions toward a discipline that advances human understanding-- ultimately, it is clear from volunteer interviews (linked in the works cited for this chapter) that they came to learn. However, they have rejected all the efforts to establish facts and share methodologies extant within the field of study, indicating that something has gone wrong.

The downside of specialization is that the explanations provided thereby are technical and not narrative-driven. Perhaps by creating an active narrative addressing the nationalism and the ideological forces at work, the characters of Osmanagic himself and his followers, and the absurdity of the situation, people might be able to see the lack of logic at work in his claims. Refutation is part of this process, but it cannot comprise the whole process, because of how much 'sense' it takes away for those people who are earnestly participating, people who feel that the process of participation *makes sense*. Rather, narrative can engage with the situation and begin to tell the story of: Why do these claims need to be true for the persons involved? Who stands to benefit? This approach might prove superior to referring only to the authority of the geologist—even though the field of geology itself does have authority over the science concerned—because invoking authority is a classic way to alienate people. Heinrich's paper is over ten years old, and people continue to flock to Visoko.

Osmanagic has the advantage of playing this both ways. He uses his own authority, which is to say, personal magnetism and stated qualifications, to lend credence to his facts and discoveries. However, he also empowers people who feel that their common sense minds have been left behind by mainstream science—they want to replace data with 'seeing' something and the fact of having 'recognized' what they have seen. The people who believe Osmanagic are choosing an appealing story that is exciting and gratifying. They gain personal power from choosing to believe, and their commitment actually increases as they devote their own resources toward the effort of excavation, as well as their own healing, activated by being onsite at this energy nexus, surrounded by other believers. It is difficult to provide laypeople with opportunities to meaningfully engage with science, but there is clearly a need for it as science is losing a narrative battle with miracles in Visoko, shared belief being a welcoming affirmation in which anyone has the capacity to become involved. Youtube commenter Radar716 says, " Wow.... finally a scientist who realizes that there is no science without the connection of spirit!!"

This analysis has not discussed Semir Osmanagic as a person, because I deliberately chose to not pursue the telling of his story so that I could tell the story of the ideals and needs of the group, which it does not appear to me that he shares personally. It should be enough to indicate that he says things like, "Dear friends! Splendid news..." as the lead-in to an interview where he and his guest claim that negative ions have been proven effective against viruses, during the Covid-19 pandemic. He uses the word 'expert' more times than I can count in the video and describes the viruses as they "dissolve instantly". The video is titled: Finally, scientific solution for the future: NEGATIVE IONS. I believe that a narrative breakdown of Osmanagic's various endeavours would be compelling and even that it might reach some of the same audience that he attracts: people who want to know more about how things work, but feel distrustful of theory as well as contemporary human motivations. For now, viewers are still attempting to participate, involving themselves in the working out of life's mysteries. Commenter Maciej Grzeskowiak says, "What do you think of scalar medallions that generate huge amount of negative ions? [sic] I am sure you know i am talking about. Greetings from Poland".

In the next section, we will look at another group of believers who spend time and money buying into an educational concept that purports to allow persons to step outside of the complicated legal and institutional labyrinth that we are born into. The concept is sold by an array of actors who package it attractively in the form of courses and lesson plans.

3. Strawman Legal Fiction /Accepted For Value Scheme

Hey, hypothetically, did you know that when you are born, a strawman is created to represent you legally? So, if your name is L Simpson, then L SIMPSON is the name of your legal fiction. Apparently, this name in capital letters has a fund attached to it, sometimes containing up to 20 million dollars, but never shared with you, the flesh and blood person living on Earth, unless you learn how to 'accept for value'. Also, according to the literature being shared about this phenomenon, all of the laws in your area pertain not to you, a living, natural person, but to your strawman, who was created by the state and must answer to it. It is supposed to be possible for you to separate yourself from your legal fiction, and live as a freeman or woman on the land, while not being part of the nation state to which your strawman belongs.

Even better, the accounts go on, because money is an illusory concept that is no longer pegged to the gold standard-- or maybe because of something that happened with the Federal Reserve in the United States, depending on where you live?-- everything you think you know about money is wrong. You can never owe someone money, because the bank account connected to your strawman is actually yours to use forever, but only if you are able to wake up to the facts of the system in which you live. There is a way to both claim the riches of your strawman account, and simultaneously to opt out of being ruled and controlled by the state. The state, after all, is also a fiction. The only real things around are people like you and me. Also sometimes God is tied into it, because the only real laws come from God, and the state is a charlatan. This is the 'accepted for value' scam.

So, if you could pay some money, and you could have access to this step by step process of disconnecting from the state, which, after all, dictates elements of your life without consent, would you choose to take the first steps toward true freedom? You've just heard the pitch to join a loose society, a belief-based group who reject elements of our governmental, financial and legal systems as absurd constructions, based upon dominance and lies.

Obviously, there are two groups involved here, with some overlap between them. There are the entities selling the legal advice, the first being guru types who swear it has worked for them, but who do not necessarily subscribe to the belief system personally. There are also the participants, who feel a sense of rightness in exercising the free choice to reject a corrupt legal system, and involve themselves to varying degrees.

In pursuit of their freedom, the 'freemen on the land', 'sovereign citizens', and taxation resistors have undergone fraud trials, been sent to prison, and had their properties foreclosed upon. What did they do wrong? According to the gurus, they probably neglected to fulfill exactly one of the steps from the step by step guide, and they should start again at the beginning. The ritual actions are proscribed and will reveal an exit from the labyrinth, at least for those who truly believe that life within the system is worthless, and who will not back down at any cost.

Attorney Colin McRoberts describes the process, " Most people who try pseudolegal arguments in court or with their creditors believe that they are adopting legitimate tactics, just as many believe that homeopathy is a serious tool for treating illness. That parallel is not surprising, as pseudoscience and pseudolaw have common roots in irrational thinking. They both appeal to people's natural fondness for self-reliance and secret knowledge. The path from curiosity toward self-destruction probably starts for many with curiosity about strange but compelling ideas – what if some of it were really true, and what's the harm in believing it when you aren't sick or in legal trouble? When the cost of error is low, the fact that snake oil doesn't work is not particularly relevant. But once the believer starts to rely on it in the real world, the spiral has begun. Someone might decide to test the waters by putting off their taxes for a little while to see if it works. Law enforcement takes years to catch up with some cases, so at first the strategy seems successful. Meanwhile, back taxes, interest and fines grow to monstrous proportions." (2016)

Of course, all of this suggests a kind of mystical alchemy, the production of an exact string of reified actions that the state is powerless to deny, though of course the will to subjugate you remains. Many of the steps involved are tied into language, and in particular legal language, which proponents identify as having binding power. Legal language is perceived by adherents to be a trick, meant to force the freeman back into submission. For instance, when the Judge at your trial asks you, "Do you understand the charges against you?", you are supposed to say, "I do not stand under them." By 'under-standing' the charges, you have apparently secretly admitted that the court has jurisdiction over you, and you have recognized the false authority of the state over you. Now you are trapped. This type of thing is what the gurus teach you in order to 'free' you from the despotic system.

The following is an excerpt from a trial transcript that took place in Alberta, Canada. A document submitted to the court is described thus: " 'Actual and Constructive Notice' from Dennis-Larry: Meads to the Bank of Canada that 'accepts for value' enclosed documents in accordance with the Uniform Commercial Code and the Bank of Canada Act to charge his 'public treasury', which is identified by his social insurance number, for $100 billion Canadian dollars or the equivalent in silver or gold." Meads also submitted a letter in which he claimed that he was under the jurisdiction of Jehovah alone, and not subject to the Crown.

The Judge, J.D. Rooke, who was there to settle a custody proceeding between Meads and his ex-wife, summed up Mead's string of claims, and his interpretation is reproduced below. Note that A4V is a short-form for 'accepted for value', part of a system whereby the natural, free man writes 'accepted for value' on all of his bills, and sends them back, assuming that the aforementioned strawman account will then pay for them.

"I will now briefly outline my understanding of the meaning of certain of Mr. Meads' actions and statements:

1.   Mr. Meads clearly subscribes to the... concept that he has two aspects, what I later discuss as the 'double/split person' concept. The German folk term "doppelganger", a kind of paranormal double, is a useful concept to describe this curious duality. Mr. Meads labels one aspect as a "person" or "corporate entity" while the other is his "flesh and blood" form.

2.   Mr. Meads also subscribes to the theory that almost any interaction with the court or state can result in a binding contract. That is why he was so apprehensive about accepting my proposal to order disclosure from Ms. Meads - that apparently benign act would allegedly bind him in contract to this Court's authority...

4.   The discussion of the alleged source of funds to discharge his child and spousal support obligations, a bank account related to his birth certificate, indicates Mr. Meads has advanced a 'money for nothing' scheme called 'A4V'."

This Canadian case has since been cited numerous times as providing precedent for understanding pseudolegal schemes, and dealing with them when they enter the courtroom. According to Laird, of the American Bar Association, freemen/sovereign citizens are, "known for the sheer volume of their filings, which can double the size of a normal docket. This can frustrate and delay courts as they consider the defendant's competence and otherwise try to minimize disruptions. With many court systems fighting heavy caseloads and budget cuts, these extra headaches are unwelcome." (quoted in McRoberts 2016)

The legal system has been forced to become familiar with the chosen terminology used to describe the freeman worldview as it is subscribed to by believers. The authority of the court, and its procedures, clearly appear arcane to the freemen on the land, who seem to sense a strangeness in the fact that a man or woman can't speak plainly and directly to their own case, being encouraged instead to hire a legal professional. Resistance toward the idea of the self as being unworthy to speak results in a feeling of 'wrongness' so familiar to anyone who has ever been part of an impersonal proceeding.

The specific teachings around having 'two aspects' appear to be a perversion of the actual concept under law of the 'legal person' or 'legal entity,' a development that allows corporations to do things like own property, and enter into binding agreements with others, by giving these entities the status of a person under law. These corporate actors are distinguished using the category of 'legal persons' because they are not 'natural persons', aka people who are physically born, live and die. Additionally, the idea of the strawman is distantly related to the Roman idea that one can renounce membership in ones family (and actually this was achieved by being bought and sold three times by ones own Father), renouncing with it the legal obligations that one had, as well as the official control of your family patriarch. Why are people choosing to make use of the concept again now?

"The recession and depression have affected everyone, be they in education, work, or retirement, or through unemployment. At the same time, people have lost trust and confidence in the financial system because so many of its activities and transactions are remote from the world of commercial realities. Those who do not work within the contracting world of financial services perceive that most transactions are based on other transactions, a sort of pyramid of transactions that occur in an artificial world, a fantasy world." (McDowall 2013) It would seem that exposure to a complex world of regulations, and the pressures of an esoteric financial system where, "money attracts money" beyond the bounds of the imagination has led to the sensation of being trapped within a society of sorcerers. The only way to have any power is to become a sorcerer, too, through a gnostic relationship with the world's forces, revealed through initiatory process as imaginary figments.

But there is a deeper issue, too. "Modern pseudolaw has roots in white supremacy and separatism." (McRoberts 2016) According to the Anti-Defamation League, "In April 1992, an angry resident of Sanilac County, Michigan, wrote a letter to the Michigan Department of

Natural Resources stating he was no longer a citizen of the corrupt political corporate State of Michigan and the United States of America and was answerable only to the 'Common Laws.'...

He was Terry Nichols, friend and accomplice of Oklahoma City Federal Building bomber Timothy McVeigh. Nichols subscribed to an unusual right-wing anti-government ideology whose adherents have in recent years increasingly plagued public officials, law enforcement officers and private citizens with a variety of tactics designed to attack the government and other forms of authority. Its members call themselves, variously, constitutionalists, freemen, preamble citizens, common law citizens and non-foreign/non-resident aliens...but most commonly refer to themselves as 'sovereign citizens.'...

Members of the sovereign citizen movement engage in a variety of seemingly bizarre activities. Nichols, for instance, several times repudiated his allegiance to federal and state governments. He tried to pay a credit card debt with a fictitious financial instrument called a 'certified fractional reserve check.' Brought into court in Michigan in 1993, he refused to walk to the front of the courtroom and denied the court's jurisdiction over him.." (ADL Press Release)

North American society has gone through many rapid changes during the process of industrialization, and high finance and speculation have come to control more about the world we live in. Ideologies that hark back to an idyllic past, utopic as they may seem at first, frequently idealize the colonial era, during which power relations were far more straightforward. White supremacists and far-right actors benefit from the freemen on the land scheme by spreading its gospel, and making money from the curious and debt-ridden along the way. Proselytizing by these actors leads to more participants, and eventually, the undermining of the government system that has allowed for their removal from power. Many proponents would replace democracy with a theocracy, including the popular priest-proponent, Paul Revere. Paul is the author of a very long blog in which he lists in minute detail the emotional experiences he had while being repeatedly incarcerated for driving without a license. Paul's refusal to bow to secular law is typical, as he longs to avoid becoming complicit in immoral activities, and sees a moral imperative in answering to God alone. Needless to say, I can speculate that Paul's desire for the larger group to be dominated and punished by God might be symbolic of the pure, cleansing nature of homogeneity. You can find a link to his writing in the works cited for this chapter.

The appeal of the 'Accepted for Value' schema is obvious in a time when the imagined freedom of the neo-liberal market has been replaced for many by a cycle of debt and low pay, and some people are unable to see the appeal of remaining connected. Folklore related to money and ways of getting it has always been commonplace, starting in the Ancient world and never abating. "Countless money-making talismans, spells, charms, and astrological incantations are available on the Internet. For as little as five dollars, you can buy a spell to ensure prosperity and success at work." (McDowall 2013)

Stories that suggest outside forces at work, influencing financial markets, are commonplace as well, whether it is a conspiracy of 'higher ups' in the government and corporate world, as referred to by proponents of 'Accepted For Value', or whether the arcane and corrupt monetary system is blamed upon the white supremacist's favourite scapegoat for all financial ills since Medieval usury laws, Jewish people. Interestingly, the alchemical obsession that led into the discipline of chemistry during that era appears out of an enduring

preoccupation with making gold out of nothing. (McDowall 2013)

The degree to which believers are involved will not always fully reflect these stated

ideologies, but surely it must be clear by now that the gurus, who are responsible for selling the

scheme, are aware of its inefficacy as a system. The 'Accepted For Value' system has been

effective at generating money for the gurus alone, as they sell course packages and make public

speaking appearances, thus spreading their ideology. Many of the gurus are distinctly and

obviously racist and homophobic, others appear as less so and attempt to cater to an audience

who want to 'opt out' for other reasons. Any participation benefits the gurus, because it

undermines the system of government they desire to affect through tax evasion, and economic

and legal havoc.

Participants lose money, as well as standing in the society that they are willing to reject,

but what their belief seems to bring them, for however fleeting an amount of time, is the

sensation of being on ethical high ground. The disenfranchisement of poorer white people (who

still hold white privilege) from automatic power in the post-colonial setting is answered by the

rejection of the system entirely, and the belief in an archaic ethic and attendant confusion about

the nature of modern life. Not every participant is likely to pick up on these overtones, and

some may be simply desperate. The notion of infinite growth, so engendered in the West,

leaves the strong feeling that scarcity is a cheap trick. Surely there must be an escape hatch

somewhere?

The distance felt between personhood and the system of finance is exemplar in the popular conspiracy theory that sunspot cycle has a persistent hold over stock market fluctuations. (McDowall 2013) This is how removed we feel ourselves to be in terms of cause and effect when we confront this massive mechanism, and I think that particular sensation is widespread, and not only found within this strange subset of believers. The logic of magic takes over when we are unable to understand or to approach.

In the next section, we will discuss the accepted notion held by another subset of believers: that the cooperation of the Universe, and your corresponding spiritual development, is a requirement in order for you to succeed with money. Similar to the 'Accepted For Value' arrangement, there are a variety of steps that must be followed precisely, and the advice of a guru is involved. Ritual cleansings of the mind and body are seemingly required. Once this process has been undergone fully, participants will almost definitely become millionaires, although only 1% of people working in the industry actually turn any significant profit according to the evidence at hand.

4. Monat and the 'Movement'

Here is the pitch: Hey girl! You can be a digital nomad, travelling the world while posting to social media and making super easy money. All you have to do is use these products that you love! You will definitely love the products, just pay a one time fee for a product pack and give them a try. The product pack comes with your own website to sell from! What we're really selling is an opportunity for freedom: that's time freedom and financial freedom. Not to mention, it comes with a group of powerful women who are so supportive and loving. We are manifesting greatness and I personally am very close to joining the Million Dollar club.

Also, it's definitely free advertising and free labour for the company, because they don't pay you anything if you're unable to make anything. You are always a customer of theirs, buying, using, and showing off the products. Although you're not forced to do so, it's really better if you post about the company every single day, and make sure not to miss the opportunity to mention the company while you discuss your amazing lifestyle, conflating it with your personal life and your individual physical beauty. Suddenly, everything good that you have to offer is only yours to offer because of this amazing company.

It goes without saying that the second part of the 'pitch' is generally left out, to be discussed later on. Early emphasis during recruitment to "this business" is upon the ease and convenience of your participation, and the relatively low required investment to take part in the opportunity. Participants alternate between referring to what they do as 'their job' and referring to joining as 'an opportunity', rather than actual employment. Much of what has been said here could refer to any MLM, but the case study that is to follow will examine the beliefs of one particular 'team' inside of Monat, via their social media. This team was chosen because it uses mental health and spiritual rhetoric to provide perceived benefit to those team members who are not succeeding at making money. Before we get into that, let's look at the MLM industry so that we can situate this particular corporation within its milieu.

In the United States, the multi level marketing industry is self-regulated by an entity called the Direct Selling Association, representing all of the related corporations as a whole. How many are there? "The DSA estimates that 1,100 MLMs are in operation in any given year but cannot be sure. 'Many companies may even come and go before they could even be 'counted'' the DSA says on its own website." (Vesoulis 2020) The Fair Trade Commission has investigated the industry as a whole in the USA, and reported that 99% of MLM participants have lost money. Basically, the aim of multi level marketing is to sell items directly to consumers, generally without storefronts, although Herbalife and Lularoe, two of the most troubled MLMs, have also allowed certain sellers to rent space. Selling tends to take place on social media, with participants either buying inventory upfront and then selling it on at a higher price point, or having customers purchase products through a link, and taking a commission percentage that varies across companies.

Ultimately, though, the aim is really to create a team through recruitment methods that play on the insecurities of others, leading them into signing on and eventually recruiting others under them. This leads to the issue of market saturation, making it almost impossible to continue signing people on, regardless of positive mindset. Those who get in early constitute the high earners, while those recruited later on face an extreme uphill battle.

As Jane Marie points out in her excellent podcast, The Dream, many women join MLMs purely out of a desire for community. These women might enjoy gathering, trying products, and positioning themselves within a social group. "The chances of financial success are so grim that the DSA president, Mariano, has called participating in MLMs an 'activity' rather than a job." (Vesoulis 2020) However, there is a dissonance here since the 'opportunity' is often sold as a means to spend more time with one's children by working from home, or as a means to exit from a dead end job. Regardless of what your problems are in life, an MLM is always the solution, if you listen to those attempting to recruit. The opportunity is presented as very broad, interacting with all areas of your life that need work and changing yourself for the better. This immersive experience that transforms that is the real product.

The following is a quoted example of a pitch for Beach Body, a health and fitness MLM with a monthly membership fee and the requirement to buy workout shakes directly from the company. First, the rep mentions in her post that she involved herself in coaching in order to find a fitness solution, and an income. Then, she says this, "But the real reason that I've stayed? Even through the ups and downs, it's this TEAM that has kept me going. The COMMUNITY of women pushing themselves to be better each day. The belief that if they can, why not me? And let's be honest, no one talks about how hard it is to make friends once you become an adult..So to the teacher who needs an outlet-- I see you. To the mom who needs a 'me time' escape-- I see you. To the girl who's looking to expand or find new circles-- I see you. To ANYONE looking for confidence and a change for themselves but doesn't know where to start-- I SEE YOU..."

It is obvious that there is an emotional side to participation in these schemes, with an emphasis on belief in the self and in the golden nature of the opportunity. I would argue that the limitless potential that participants are told they must believe in, and the discord that results when funds are spent, but nothing is coming in, is dealt with within the scheme by blaming the individual for not doing enough, personally. Mindset is often blamed for what is definitely a structural problem in a field where failure is basically guaranteed. This is a familiar evocation for some participants, for whom belief in the 'prosperity gospel' is part of North American life. This concept is a, "transdenominational doctrine that emphasizes that God grants material prosperity, good health, or relief from sickness to those who have enough faith (Anderson 2004; Gifford 2007; Pew Forum 2006). Scholars have also referred to this as the 'health and wealth gospel' or 'prosperity theology'. Simply put, this belief conveys a potent and appealing message: God wants you to thrive."(Schieman + Jung 2012) I would argue that this doctrine is central to a capitalistic mindset.

Monat is a newer company who has shifted away from many traditional aspects of direct sales, including inventory loading and monthly membership fees. Their compensation plan, however, still has many issues. Their ranking system, on which earnings depend, has minimum sales requirements each month and requires re-qualification monthly, meaning that a rank attained can be easily lost. Industry saturation (too many sellers in one area or niche) is never considered, and there are no caps on new 'market partners' as they join on. Monat also includes the classic 'car scheme' in which you qualify to purchase a white Cadillac, but the corporation has you sign your name on the lease, and pays you out in the amount of your monthly payment, but *only* each month that you continue to qualify according to your current rank. If you lose team members, for instance, your numbers will likely be affected, and you will be on the hook for your own car payment, since you no longer technically qualify.

Monat market partners sell hair and skin care, but above all it sells the recycled image of the successful woman (and images of ritual cleansing). Its site states, vaguely, "We are successful when we help others be successful. We are happy when we help others be happy." The site is careful not to be crass and make specific claims about excessive earnings publicly, as FTC warning letters have recently spooked many in the industry. Instead, Monat has positioned itself as a caring partner to you, with the philanthropic aim of making your life better. Their text slide reads, "It is our mission to help people everywhere enjoy beautiful, healthy, fulfilling lives through our exceptional, naturally based products, a fun and rewarding business opportunity, and a culture of family, service, and gratitude." Nice! Emphasis should be put on the use of the word 'fun' for later contrast with the statements made by market partners who are in conversation with their own teams. The word 'fun' is a gatekeeper, welcoming people in as they are recruited, and then disappearing from view.

Because of the nature of the data that I gathered (it comes from market partner Instagram pages and Youtube recordings of team calls), I will not be printing my media sources here. My sources would reveal the identities of the participants, and while all information reported here is publicly listed by the market partners, it is my fear that they will experience negative repercussions should this publication direct visitors to their social media who intend to confront them. My list of sources is available for academic study upon request for those who are interested in gathering data on the industry-- specifically it will be available only for those who are affiliated with an institution of learning.

I do not consider the market partners to be participating human subjects and consider myself to be investigating the narratives generated and publicly presented during MLM participation only. I looked into the ethics of social media based research and I have been guided by standard practices, exemplified in the following: "A human subject is defined by federal regulations as a living individual about whom an investigator obtains data through interaction with the individual or identifiable private information. If the following conditions are met, access to the SMW is public; information is identifiable, but not private; and information gathering requires no interaction with the person who posted it online, and then presumably the proposed project does not constitute the human subjects research. For example, an observational study of YouTube videos involves publicly posted and available content accessible to any Internet user. In this case, the information is not private, and it does not require any interaction with the subject to access it.

Observational research may also meet the criteria for exemption from...review if the study involves observation of public information regarding individual human subjects. Exempt research includes research involving the observation of public behavior, except when information obtained is (a) recorded in such a manner that subjects can be identified either directly or through the identifiers linked to the subjects, or (b) any disclosure of subjects' responses outside the published research that could reasonably place the subjects at risk of criminal or civic liability, or be damaging to the subjects' financial standing, employability, or reputation." (Moreno et al 2013)

I view the market partners whose statements I will reproduce here as victims of Monat first and foremost. It might appear clear that their beliefs have the potential to cause harm to others, and in that sense they are implicated here anonymously, solely as an example of participant behaviours stemming out of a system of shared belief. The appearance of extreme wealth is inculcated among participants by their uplines, aka the 1% of market partners who are managing to turn a profit, as well as by the corporation, which calls itself the #1 luxury hair care line in the world.

What I have discovered through reading and watching the content of one team of market partners operating out of Ontario, Canada, is a trend of tying in vague spirituality, the idea of emotional readiness, and engagement with trauma in the hopes of being rewarded monetarily by the Universe for having done so. This emotional exegesis is the 'activity' for which the market partners have gathered, and it sustains their involvement even when monetary gain may be postponed. In order to gather thematic content, I transcribed information from HGTV videos posted to Instagram, live Team Calls, stories, and textual messages accompanying that content. All of this content, including the team calls, has been posted publicly, although there are clearly degrees of involvement and various materials are keyed to each degree. At the first stage, meant for those people outside of the current team, money is talked about a lot. Emphasis is placed on the opportunity as a means to an end, an effective way to gather funds.

This quote comes from one of the team leaders, Leader #1 and is directed at the general public, the recruiting pool that is currently outside of the group. "I'm not talking about some random commission thing that you can do on the side. I'm not talking about a little bit of commission here and there. I'm talking about life changing money. So...Making money is a weird taboo thing that not a lot of people talk about, but I want to talk about it...With this company you can make lots of money, way before. I make more than most influencers with hundreds of thousands of followers and I have not even three thousand followers yet...I'm working with one company, and that company pays me so much more than I could've imagined...

It started with, just wanting enough to get my nails done every week, and now I want to be a millionaire by the time I'm 25. We have something called the Million Dollar club, and basically every paycheque that we make with Monat goes towards this kind of million dollar thing and they calculate it up and when you've made a million dollars with the company, you are able to say that you're Million Dollar Club. And so that is the goal, for me, that I'm working on every day, that I'm focusing on and that I am running towards...I'm looking for financial freedom, for me, in my twenties....If you have no idea what you want to do, but you want to set yourselves up in your twenties, you want to save for the rest of your life and make an income that has you purchasing a house by yourself before you're 30, that sort of stuff."

Notice that here the emphasis is placed on what the company can do for you, setting yourself up well, making sure that you are provided for and setting large sales goals in the hopes of large payouts. Keywords are 'luxe', 'premium', and 'rich'. However, once you're behind the curtain (again, everything I have used in my research has been posted publicly online, but the various publications seem to be geared to the expectations of a few different audiences according to their degree of participation), Leader #1, in her team training call, admits to capitalizing on fear, describing herself as 'gauging the fear level' of new recruits and advising the leaders she is training to do the same, rather than to search for the type of person they believe will be most likely to find success. Rather, the recruitment pool should be as broad as possible, by incorporating ubiquitous self doubt into the process.

She tells her leaders in her team training call, about new recruits: "I literally ask them what their fears are, what their hesitations would be...Nobody believes in themselves before they do this... If you believe in this person, they will sign up with you, you will be their mentor. If you've not taken yourself from a place of 'I can't do this' to a place of 'I can do this' and you need to have had some kind of groundbreaking fear and come out of it resilient...It's not about someone with three million followers who signs up people, that's not what Modern Nature is about. It's about, anyone can do this. "

The Leaders openly recognize their spiritual teaching as setting their team apart from others, asking their team on a training call, "What makes us different?" Leader #1, in answer, begins to offer counsel and direction, emphasizing first of all the need for vulnerability. This is key, because willingness to participate in group counselling and to start a process of transformation through joining the belief group is the difference between 'success' and 'failure' for new recruits, at least as the team defines it. You are successful if you have allowed yourself to be transformed. The only way to be unsuccessful is to remain closed off, not integrate with the belief group, and quit.

Leader 1 says the following: "We are very spiritual, we work from a spiritual place and we add that into our business on a daily basis. I'm going to give you some spiritual practices for you to do, very basic... when people start to run with it, and their [Instagram] stories start to pop off, I personally believe that happens when people don't carry their baggage and their bullshit into their stories, and into their business. I have ways to deal with that, and I'm going to give you a little meditation to do going forward. It's called Shadow work...Something that you can do, is work through your stuff."

She goes on to offer direct counselling, through the provision of an exercise to bring up traumatic memories from the subconscious, "Something I do, is I set a timer for 10 minutes and I just sit or lie down...say to yourself, I want whatever memory or past traumatic event that's blocking me to pop up, to come up for me and let me know what I want to heal and move forward, usually an event will pop up, whether that be business related, whether that be relationship related, whatever related, something is going to pop up for you, and that' s going to let you feel that emotion...We can spew out all of the personal development stuff, but if we haven't related it to our past, me and (Name of Leader 2) really feel that is what is holding you back in your business, or keeping you from that flow in your business...You're working hard, you're posting in your stories every day, you're trying to be authentic, you're doing the personal development work, why the hell isn't it happening? What is wrong? Why am I not getting the DMs [direct messages from prospects and customers] that I want...

I personally feel that it's not your time yet, and you have something to work out...Understand that it's not time for you yet, but there is something that you can do, which is to work on your shit...You're running faster than yesterday, you've left behind some of your baggage and you're running...You might think that you put something to bed, but you haven't...You have to be open to the fact that something you thought was healed, hasn't yet."

This last part is very convenient. If I'm open to the fact that, even when I think I'm feeling okay, any slowdown of my business is definitely related to my trauma, then I can remain in infinite regress, trying over and over to be 'ready'. My readiness will be proven only by business success through sales, and until then I should continue to assume that something from my past is not resolved. This is a very dangerous mentality. These 'blockages' become the focus, with proper remuneration fading into the background and becoming less important.

Leader #2 goes on in the same vein, describing the types of issues that market partners may have experienced that could be currently sabotaging their success. "It could be as simple as a NO that you got that really stung...Or not having the support of your parents, or your best friend...It might not be something within the business but it's being pulled into the business... we do think it's important for everyone to do this background work...Because we think that if you've dealt with the past, you can deal with today, you can deal with the nos, you can deal with the struggle and the hard months, and the sleepless nights, and all the things that might come along with this business...A lot of the personal development we do is very positive based...but I get overwhelmed when I have to be that perfect entrepreneur...Doing the back end of what you've gone through in your business, going through the hardships and coming to peace with it...when you think about a situation, do you get that lump in your tummy?"

Leader #2 then brings up the concept of a dark why and light why. Your dark why consists of what you do not want, essentially, your fears. "Do you not want to be living with your parents? Do you not want to be in debt? What's keeping you awake at night? Not because you want it, but because you don't want it." Notice here the continued use of fear. Fear is never mentioned during public recruitment on Instagram, but constantly discussed with the in-group on the (still public, but used by members) Youtube channel. Also, notice that the very notion of the business has been changed around while the market partners have been busy looking away into their own psyches, undergoing these quasi counselling practices as directed by their uplines. The business, which was sold as a freedom-enhancing opportunity to be rich, has turned into struggle, hard months, and sleepless nights. It has a redeeming quality though, which is the group itself, and membership in it. The group shares their traumas with one another, which emphasizes their bond, and moves them toward what appears to be emotional, cathartic experiences.

The Leaders share their struggles explicitly, and they expect the same in return. Leader #1 shares on the team call, using the theme of providence, divine timing, and the blessing within the struggle: "There was more for me to do internally. To lead a team, to mentor ranks and director ranks, I needed to fall down and do that internal work. I scream cried for all December, I had panic attacks upon panic attacks because I had lost everything I never wanted...Failure has to happen. I'm going to be bringing this onto my stories...there's a shift in just realizing that. Suddenly I was able to talk about Million Dollar Club (note, she is referring to the video quoted initially, directed at the public and all about making money)... It's not that you don't want it bad enough. You do the work and you show up to your stories...It's not your time yet, and you have more to move in. Call it karma, call it karmic debt, look inside yourself...It's not your time yet."

Leader #2 begins to share, describing the way that her naivete worked to her advantage at the start of her business because she had not yet absorbed 'the negativity of others'. Once she started to hear bad things about the business model, she began to hesitate, and she stopped succeeding and began to go backwards in her business, until finally she 'got her light back.' This is a common statement by MLM uplines, who will do just about anything to convince their team members to avoid messaging that might cause them to question the company. All such messaging is really 'negativity'. She also reinforces the message of looking for signs to determine whether it is your time to succeed according to divine timing, with an emphasis on self-work in order to be worthy: "You have to work through your shit if it's going to be your time."

Leader #2 goes deeper into these themes on a second team call. "Showing up with confidence gives people watching the idea that, if i want to join with anyone, I want to join with her...It all comes down to getting over your own shit and past your own blocks...Do you feel like a leader? Do you feel you have what it takes to lead people to success? If not, maybe that's what you need to work on....It's about turning ordinary people into extraordinary people..." Of course, this sounds very positive. Understand the that the bait and switch that is happening is nothing more than making losing money, more engaging. She is at least offering something to the market partners under her, something definite that they will receive: attention, transformation, emotional breakdown and consequent rebirth. Money is no longer mentioned. Instead, the market partner, who is being trained as a counsellor in her own right as she becomes an upline for others, becomes a powerful person to others, whose emotions she must engage with, "You have the power to make or break people, that's a lot of responsibility. You need to hold them with care."

We can see, when we examine social media messaging coming from downlines in the same team, that these messages have trickled down, and that the market partners at those levels have been trained to blame themselves and look within if success is not forthcoming. Beliefs about the universe providing for only those who are ready are evident here. This is a great method which serves to explain frustration and struggle in the business, in a way that does not threaten the overall structural arrangement that causes earnings not to reflect market partner efforts.

Here is a message taken from a post by a downline market partner who had just received a promotion, complete with a celebratory pin. The promotion was small, and it had been a long time coming, but the message indicates that the market partner has identified therapeutically with the situation, just as she has been taught to. All of the ups and downs in Monat are ordained and meant to imbue her with specific qualities. The struggles themselves, and the spiritual development that has accompanied them, are the experience, the chosen 'activity' believed to improve the self and the world. Monat market partners believe in the company.

"You know, hitting this goal was so big and it was so unobtainable. But when I finally got there, I knew that I needed to take the time that I did and that I needed to grow the way that I did to, you know, get this little pin. Which, for you guys, probably doesn't signify much. But this pin shows me that I don't give up. This shows me that I believe in myself wholeheartedly, and just because something wasn't easy, I didn't stop. Do you guys know how hard it is to watch other people get the things that you feel that you deserve so much...I should be at MMB, I should be that rank, I am such a leader. But I don't have this, and I don't have that, and my team doesn't see the same vision. All of that rounded up together...but divine timing, guys. It didn't happen six months ago because I wasn't ready for it. It didn't happen a year ago, because I wasn't ready for it...I was angry about that, I didn't move out when I was eighteen, that's not the path I'm supposed to be on. And no matter what greater force you believe in: God, the universe, yourself, whatever it is, divine timing is so real. You are where you are for a reason. You are where you are in your life for a greater reason than we can even comprehend.

I don't have my Cadillac yet, I am not, you know, travelling the world every month yet, obviously with things going on (she is referring to the covid-19 pandemic), but because that's not where I'm supposed to be in my life... For 18 months, I was supposed to struggle, I was supposed to want to give up, I was supposed to have my entire business crumble beneath me and me to have to rebuild and start everything up again. I was supposed to go through all the growth, all the tears, all the anxiety, that was all meant to happen to get to this point. Because if I just got this when I felt like I deserved it, it wouldn't be as rewarding. This shows me that I will not give up, that I want more for myself, and that I will continue to get more for myself."

This statement shows that, through the power of belief, this market partner has divorced notions like the amount she feels she should make based on the amount of work she put in, and such things as the duration of her work, from expected remuneration. Instead, she associates achieving milestones, like the promised Cadillac, with God's plan, or a predestined path, along which she will proceed when she is 'meant to'. The amount of time this market partner will participate in the opportunity/belief group will likely increase through this direct association of business hardships with virtue and spiritual development, thus making money for their upline, and the company itself, for longer.

Evidently, the studied team has not always had a spiritual/counselling based approach that incorporates divine timing. At an earlier stage, the Leaders had, perhaps, a more general approach, with Leader 1 stating that she had formerly recruited heavily from sponsored ads. This technique was not as effective, as she had many market partners join who would then usually abruptly leave, probably because they were not making money. She opens up about this directly in a training video, meant to serve members of her team who are moving into leadership roles over their own downlines, when she says, "I can't lead them because I don't know them, I didn't know I needed to know them. In December my whole team falls off...because I'm sort of begging and pleading to work with me...I didn't click with them, because we didn't have a connection...You need to start selling the connection. They need to sign up because they want to work with you...Building relationships, that is building a sustainable business."

She admits to probing new team members for vulnerabilities by asking: What can I help you with? What are you going through right now? The answer to any issue will always be the Leader(s), who are now your mentors and friends and will reconcile you with God, failure, and success, so long as you continue to sell and buy shampoo from the company they work for, and to post images of your ritual cleansings.

We will now look at a sample of comments from members of the team, describing the experience of joining, and consequently, entering the belief group although they would likely not term it as such:

-I am so grateful for the amazing community I am now able to call friends

-The best feeling ever. Instant family vibes. We are not business partners, we are sisters basically. I never thought I would be a part of a worldwide community of strong, independent women, but now I am and I love it here.

-Right when i got added, I was flooded with welcomes and positive energy! Everyone on the team is so empowered and inspiring.

-Literally felt like such a positive space, with unlimited support, and a great way to meet new people

-I was welcomed with open arms and love! you girls have been one of the best things ever to happen to me.

-I've been met with such love and light ever since I joined this team, and I can't imagine my life without it.

There are a great deal more responses, all replete with terms like, 'sisters' and 'community', and phrases like, 'positive vibes,' and 'build each other up.' Everything is summed up perfectly in the second comment. They, the MPs, are not business partners. They are a spiritual counselling group that also enriches those at the top monetarily. Those at the bottom receive the benefits stated, in the form of relationships, positive reinforcement, and celebration of struggle, and involvement in individual and shared traumas in the interest of healing and providence.

What is pretty clear is that, if you are being paid, you don't also require faith. A traditional job trades corporate money for your time. It isn't required that you involve your whole being, or that you become vulnerable and willing to delve into your past hurts. Yes, there may be damaging occurrences at a job, and there may be uplifting experiences in the course of employment. But, these things are secondary. Your employer doesn't *need* to offer these deeper experiences, because they offer funds as the reason for your presence. In the absence of definite compensation, an array of emotional offerings have been generated.

The DSA President would imply that it is actually the market partners at fault here, implicating that the true nature of the business is known to them, but that they are choosing consciously to suggest that there are millions to be made. "DSA president Joseph Mariano says some sellers have inflated the potential rewards of investing in their companies. 'You inevitably have a few overzealous people saying things that perhaps they shouldn't,' he says. 'When you have a vulnerable population of people who have lost their jobs or are concerned about losing their jobs, the fact of the matter is...direct selling is generally a modest supplemental income opportunity. It's not something that is going to make you rich." (Vesoulis 2020)

I would argue that, instead, the rhetoric of richness comes directly from above. Why is there a Million Dollar Club at all, for instance, if Monat is not attempting to say that you might make a million dollars? The type of culture that we found is just this particular team's way of compensating for that which the company is not actually offering to the vast majority, that is, life changing money. It is another form of symbolic appeasement, used in order to avoid the far more costly and rewarding resource-based appeasement.

In the next section, we will examine the mythic (symbolic appeasement again!) notion that the court system is impartial. Beforehand, if you are not familiar with police conduct, please read about the conduct of the police according to reputable sources, as well as anecdotal comments from affected persons. Remember that the police feed people into the federal, state/provincial and local levels of the court system, so that the arrival of persons in that system (and onto the books as casualties of police violence) varies according to their ethnic makeup in North America. You can start here:

http://www.ohrc.on.ca/en/public-interest-inquiry-racial-profiling-and-discrimination-toronto-police-service/collective-impact-interim-report-inquiry-racial-profiling-and-racial-discrimination-black

Or if you are reading the print copy, search for the following to find the report: A Collective Impact: Interim report on the inquiry into racial profiling and racial discrimination of Black persons by the Toronto Police Service.

5. Shared Delusions: Belief in the Impartiality of the Courts

The equality attending the public realm is necessarily an equality of unequals

who stand in need of being "equalized" in certain respects

and for specific purposes. -Hannah Arendt

It goes without saying that we are having a powerful and tragic experience in North America right now in spring of 2020, as anti police brutality movement Black Lives Matter reacts to the incarceration state and its attendant racism, and Covid-19 dis-proportionally affects black communities. With this on our minds, let's turn to the court system. The courts are meant to be impartial. This is a statement of belief, however, and many are not naive enough to take it on its face. Even the related statement that, "human beings are capable of being impartial while on duty as professionals" is a statement of belief, as yet unproven. Both of these are statements form part of the nexus of common group beliefs.

So much of the Western ethos seems to come from the wish for objectivity, if only as a facade. All of these professions, doctors, judges, scientists, officials, all apparently with the ability to dislocate from their human personality and inherent biases. When it comes to this shared belief, it is European/ North American society as a whole making up the group. Many, if not all, racialized people within that society, however, probably know that this supposed objectivity is not actually possible because of the racism that they experience institutionally, even through the lens of science, both historically and in this era. Many women are unlikely to imagine that impartiality is possible either, because of the different and lower quality treatment they receive from professionals, as compared with the treatment of men as received from those same professionals. Though there is dissent, most people operate as if they believe in impartiality in practice. It is treated as a virtue where it is found, which indicates its existence as an ever present standard, despite the abstract nature of professional objectivity as a concept.

Let's look at the courts. I'm going to lean heavily on Shapiro for this first part, because I believe he presents an accurate and historically precise picture of the court system in his book, Courts: a Comparative and Political Analysis (1981). Trials began as literal trials, often painful tests to determine God's favour. God's favour was complex, involving sinking and burning and whether or not a wound festered or it healed and so on. They were presided over by someone whose job it was to administer the test and judge the result. Shapiro described basic trials as, "triadic conflict resolution by an important figure, or just a person who is either way usually chosen by the parties or confirmed by them." Think of King Solomon serving as a judge in the Bible, with disputants coming to him.

Shapiro goes on, "Once confidence of divine intervention in routine trials is reduced, problems of credibility and weight of evidence arise. Few human societies have found probabilistic treatment of evidence morally satisfying...Most trial courts, of course, pretend to a certainty that they know is not there...In the 17th century notions of probability or relative certainty seem to develop side by side in theology, science, and law. In Western societies a trial gradually comes to be seen as an empirical investigation designed to determine the weight of evidence on each side rather than as an attempt to discover the absolute truth. This progression from the search for absolute truth by divine intervention up to modern notions of balance of evidence should not be taken, however, as a necessary or universal phenomenon. Ethnographic materials show us some tribal judges who seek to assert definitive fact finding capacity while others openly admit to weighing or balancing the evidence and picking the more convincing story."

Our courts today do a little bit of both. Ultimately, a narrative is chosen-- a version of things that becomes the official story that is entered into our record. The legal system, once proof was put onto the table, has had a variety of interpretations of who must prove what, and to what degree of certainty. "The presumption of innocence is not some fixed truth but a declaration of social policy," according to Shapiro, placing the burden of proof on the state in order to promote the rights of the accused. How does it work in practice?

In practice, around 90% of criminal cases in the United States are resolved via a plea bargain, meaning that, since the police are more likely to target and accuse racialized people during investigation and routine patrols, it is these people who largely end up convicted. The guilty plea usually removes the right to ask for an appeal, but in the cases where it is granted, sentencing is usually not under review-- only whether the law as interpreted was correctly applied. "These three factors combine to create a major anomaly, at least within the Western political and administrative tradition." (Shapiro 1981) Overly harsh sentencing, then, can't be dealt with through the appeal. The court system cannot be impartial if decisions around guilt are decided by sentencing the bulk of arrested persons, with the facts of cases primarily not even examined thoroughly, with no possibility for appeal. If the appeals process doesn't serve the accused, who does it serve?

Shapiro asserts that, "appeal allows the loser to continue to assert his rightness in the abstract without attacking the legitimacy of the legal system or refusing to obey the trial court." So, it serves as a form of symbolic appeasement, especially in civil cases-- it does not seem to function as well in criminal cases. Also, the process of appeal directs difficult questions up toward the top, enhancing centralization and helping to establish uniformity. "The top insists on being the ultimate level of appeal because it serves its purposes, not those of a losing disputant...appellate institutions are more fundamentally related to the political purposes of central regimes than to the doing of individual justice...When we focus on the lawmaking activities of courts, we can see that appeal is a mechanism that sorts out unresolved issues of public policy and moves them towards the top for decision." (1981)

Essentially, Shapiro suggests that the prototype of agreeing to refer a dispute to a chosen third party for mediation, assumed not to have any stake in the game, has been replaced by three interested parties: the two disputants, and the state. If the chosen party was assumed to be impartial, it was simply because both disputants gave him the nod, likely not because it was assumed that he had the power to be fully objective. He or she may have been acceptable to both as an impressive, reasonable or intelligent enough person, for instance. The judge, on the other hand, is a representative of the state and its ideology. It is the state who employs the Judge, that state which has not been chosen by the accused party, the ideology of which may be directly opposed to the interests of the accused party. It seems as if, "the notion of an 'independent judiciary', which is central to the conventional prototype of courts, is simply an elaborate rationalization for the substitution of coercion for consent. The state now imposes a judge on the parties. The judge is openly and admittedly a state official. It is repeatedly asserted, nonetheless, that he is 'independent'." (Shapiro) The jury, remember, is rarely present. They enter only for criminal trials if plea deals are not taken. The jury, also, is not considered to be impartial. Both sides try to stack it with people they believe might be more likely to buy into their narrative.

Additionally, judges make law, where their decisions are binding, and they do this on behalf of the state, causing an additional issue in some trials. In cases of judicial law making, disputants have no way of knowing in advance the result of their trials resolution on the law itself. They cannot enter into the trial knowing that they have been in compliance with the law, since the ruling had not even occurred at the time of their transgression. Also, the numbers presented by Shapiro in the eighties have actually gotten worse, with even more plea deals during criminal cases in evidence than there were before. See the works cited for this chapter to explore further.

Now that we have the issues with impartiality presented clearly by Shapiro and extrapolated on through my lens, let's ask ourselves if we're dealing with a purely Western problem by looking at two short examples, the localist court system of the Chagga people, and the International Court of Justice. The Chagga court system legitimizes itself as representative of brotherhood, seen as the highest virtue in that society. The ICJ is legitimized by nations who, as in the early prototype, agree voluntarily to fall under its jurisdiction. Are these courts fair?

The Chagga people hold kinship paramount, and as a result, fights between brothers have the potential to rend the social fabric. As a result, because of the disturbing symbolic implications, fights always need to take place because of the inherent badness of one brother, and NOT because the idea of harmony is untenable in practice. "If such a controversy is not allowed to expand to involve factions, but is instead contained, limited, and narrowed to the persons directly involved, its divisive danger to the community is minimized...if everyone is mobilized against one of the disputants, who then becomes a unanimously rejected individual." (Moore 1969) The Chagga court, helpfully, treats accusations on a single-occasion basis, thus refusing to present a clear cut explanation for its own actions and decisions throughout time, treating them instead as one-offs, self contained rulings.

But how does Chagga society decide who must be rejected? "In such situations, the matter of power and popularity of the attacked person is very important to the outcome...But it cannot be admitted that this is so, lest such imply great uncertainties about the moral rules that are supposed to lie behind the social order." (Moore 1969) In Chagga society, because of complex inheritance rules and a land shortage, the middle brother is generally socially weaker than the other two, who have clearer future roles. The middle brother, then, is more often related to accusations of wrongdoing over a long period. His wife is more likely to be accused of witchcraft, and he is more likely to be accused of ungenerous behaviour. His lack of generosity, though, is likely resultant from his lower social and economic status.

In time, the reputation of the middle brother is ruined as the result of inevitable losses suffered in his neighbourhood court, where, due to his unimportant position in the family, he is seen as extraneous to the functioning of the group as a whole. The middle brother has a tendency to lose disputes, unless he has some other attribute that makes him better liked. The court is made up of local people, all known to one another, patriarchs, kinsmen, and neighbours. Elders serve as the judges, and all of the local persons are meant to ensure that rulings are followed, as a collective. (Moore 1969)

These appearances in the local court, "are part of a process of ranking. In the circumstances of the Chagga land shortage, they may be part of a desperate elimination contest in which the community must slough off some members to survive. The sloughing off of a community 'brother' must be rationalized and made congruent with the ideology of community solidarity. If a community must reject one of its own and yet extol the values of community and brotherhood and mutual obligation, it must somehow identify the rejected person as a justifiable exception to these common commitments. Rejection of a member must be turned into an affirmation of community." (Moore 1969) All of this seems strangely familiar, doesn't it?

Framed in this way, it's easy to see that the Chagga court system in Kilimanjaro was not impartial, at the time of Moore's study. It is important to note, however, that rhetoric around the court insisted upon its fairness, and the fact that it holds every brother as valuable. The unspoken fact that crowded conditions on Chagga farms were making it impossible to retain all of the 'brothers' lurked in the background, unacknowledged by those who shared these beliefs.

Let's move on to the International Court of Justice, an institution that I find fascinating. The jurisdiction of the ICJ is on a voluntary basis, making it more of a holdover from the pure triadic form of conflict resolution cited by Shapiro. There are three ways in which nations can agree to it. It can be built into a treaty agreement to resolve future conflicts, it can be applied due to 'special agreement', where both states resolve to accept and appear there, and there is also compulsory jurisdiction, where states agree to appear if called, in return for the ability to require other ratifying states to appear when summoned. Decisions are not so much traditionally *binding*, so much as they are *occurring, proceeding* visibly in the public sphere, as nations can actually pull out of cases and remove themselves from compulsory jurisdiction at will. (Posner 2005)

The results of each case end with the verdict-- the court does not monitor the situation afterwards, except in a few special cases involving the Security Council supervising, for instance, the departure of troops after a border dispute. Donoghue tells us that, "when we evaluate the effectiveness of an international court, we must be careful to set aside expectations that derive from training in our respective national legal systems....The institutions that exist alongside a national court, which influence our ideas about a court's role in shaping behavior, simply do not have international corollaries...There is no world legislative or executive branch and, as is often said, there is no international sheriff. It follows that the mechanism whereby ICJ judgments influence state behavior must be different from the mechanisms operating within a national legal system." (2014)

An interesting paper by Paulson (2004) suggests that the ICJ has a broad symbolic influence, that the threat of it (in a public relations context) encourages arbitration so that states might resolve differences without having recourse to it, and that it can be looked at as a way to communicate broadly with the world the position of the state-- and that it can be used to increase the speed of arbitration, which otherwise may take place in a far more informal fashion, with greater risk of war. States can use rulings or their own contentions, such as accusing the other litigant of non compliance, as news. The court accepting the case, even where the other party refuses to appear, can shame that nation as they seem to be flouting the law.

In cases like 1994's dispute between Libya and Chad over the Aouzou strip, Libya appeared to use loss in court, compliance and withdrawal from the strip as a public relations measure. In Cameroon v. Nigeria: Equatorial Guinea Intervening, Nigeria was chastised by a number of countries and by the press after refusing to accept the judgment, having agreed to abide by it beforehand. (Paulson 2004)

Now that we understand the unique nature of the court, let's get into whether or not it seems to render impartial judgments. The first consideration is the composition of the court. There are generally 15 judges, although this number can vary slightly, and usually a judge from each of the litigant countries is added, if they are not represented. "Whereas judges vote in favour of a party about 50 percent of the time when they have no relationship with it, that figure rises to 85-90 percent when the party is the judge's home state." (Posner 2005) Luckily, the large number of judges means that the outcome is little affected by the obvious allegiance of each judge to the nation who placed him or her on the court.

Security Council members retain a seat each at all times, meaning that the court has near constant representation of judges from America, France, Britain and Russia. Certain amounts of seats are assigned to each region of the world, with two from Latin America, Western Europe and its former colonies in North America, NZ and Australia taking five, Africa taking three, three for Asia, and two for Eastern Europe. Clearly, this arrangement leaves a lot to be desired. The rotation of states leaves out a variety of players, meaning that, "larger and wealthier states such as Germany, Japan and Canada are more likely to have representation than are smaller states." (Posner 2005)

The other issue is that the court more closely resembles Western legal systems, rather than, say Islamic ones. Certain countries are more likely to be familiar with and in agreement with legal precepts used there, especially countries which have secular legal systems in particular. Those who see the law as grounded in the authority of God are probably not likely to perceive the court as having jurisdiction over them. The court constantly includes colonial powers, allowing them to keep virtually permanent seats, at the expense of others. In the 1966 South West Africa case, South Africa controlled territory in present day Namibia. Various states including Ethiopia and Liberia took issue with their continued administration of these areas, probably because South Africa, as an apartheid state, had an ethic considered to be abhorrent by others in the region. The ICJ agreed to take the case, but after a changeover of judges (these occur every three years), had a change of heart and refused, resulting in a loss in confidence among the African states, who agreed among themselves to cease using the court for a time to protest its colonial affiliations. (Posner 2005)

Let's take a look at the meat and potatoes of Posner's results, linked in the works cited for this chapter if you'd like to get further into the nuances of his data. His paper posited that judges were likely biased not only toward their own states, as already evidenced, but also towards those states which most resembled them. After controlling for a number of factors, states are defined as belonging to "blocs—on the basis of region, wealth, culture, military and political alliances, and similar factors—so that we can determine whether judges are biased in favor of state parties that belong to the same bloc as the judges' home states...We find strong evidence that...judges favor states whose wealth level is close to that of the their own states, and weaker evidence that judges favor states whose political system is similar to that of their own states." (2005)

This is hardly surprising, since it is well known among those who study persuasion and influence that perceived similarity is key to establishing an affinity with an individual or group. Even in the absence of a personal relationship, perceived similarity can have an effect on perception. (Cialdini 1985) Such favouring of litigants who are from similar economic or political systems as the judge is likely unconscious, although it is also possible that certain judges are instructed directly to bolster national relations with certain litigants, having been appointed by dictators, totalitarian systems, or monarchies with entrenched power. (Posner 2005) I assume that, for the most part, judges are trying to interpret the law to the best of their ability. But, impartiality implies far more than that, being a rejection of any explicit or implicit bias. Additionally, the biases of those members of the court who are entrenched and appear often are likely to have more of an effect on court decisions overall. The security council countries are more of a position to exert influence, meaning that it is those favoured by security council countries who will benefit from their bias, when it shows itself.

It should be evident here that impartiality comforts us, but that it rarely shows itself the way it would if it were one of the dominant qualities operating within our institutions of justice. Often, they operate to benefit those with entrenched power. The parties, who receive these benefits, of course, vary between systems. By identifying them around you, you can identify the people who really decide for the group what is right and what is wrong. Remember that, "tendencies are morally and legally neutral. It is the existence of laws and taboos that qualifies their expression in certain ways as delinquent, or criminal, and otherwise dis-social or antisocial from the point of view of the particular society and culture in question. Adaptation to the demands and prohibitions of any social organization requires certain physical, temperamental, and intellectual capacities dependent upon the values protected by that society through law and custom." (Tibbetts 2018)

If affinity, kinship formed by shared qualities, is demonstrably at play in the highest court in our world, it should not be doubted that it is in play in the courts operating in your area. Who is in power? Who is most similar to those in power? The court system will favour those persons.

6. Culture Bound Syndromes

The medical profession, as well as the respective society that it serves, are both invested in shared beliefs that make the process of curing intelligible. Being sick is a concept across cultures, although the perceived causes and the remedies vary. Interestingly, presentation of sickness, the way someone who is sick should look, act, and express that sickness, is also extremely variant. Expression of sickness needs to be acceptable enough to be properly 'read' as sickness, and diagnosed by the medical system in which the sufferer finds him or herself, in order to be dealt with. Helman tells us that, "different social and cultural groups utilize different languages of distress in communicating their suffering to others, including to doctors...The presentation of illness may also be learned from doctors, as well as from the media, especially by patients with chronic diseases. They learn to display the 'typical' clinical picture that the doctors are looking for." (1997) Of course, there will always be variations among groups.

Broadly, among Chinese patients, for instance, physical pains are more likely to be used in order to express mental anguish, and to avoid any unnecessary stigma during the process of doing so. The system of the human body as conceived within Traditional Chinese Medicine is not ruled by the body-mind duality. All of the emotional, affective qualities of the body correspond with certain other clusters of physical symptoms, and thus depression or anxiety can be diagnosed in a fashion through speaking about these, without having to divulge anything beyond this coded language, understood within the context of that culture, but creating issues in diasporic care, where it often cannot be 'read'. (Helman 1997) It is evident that there is more going on, beyond the investigation into cause and cure-- something abstract, laden with meaning. The organs themselves are understood not only physically, but also associatively.

These cultural conceptions about sickness and health are not only along geographic lines, but can also relate to subcultures. Within Scientology, for instance, it is not acceptable to act sick at all, or to express physical symptoms of any sort. Any expression of symptoms indicates that you are a potential source of problems, and may be a danger to the group. A real Scientologist, living by the precepts set forth, would not see any need for sickness, and would eschew it. The proper treatment is to figure out which overt act the sick person has committed, but it would be better if they addressed it themselves. An 'overt act' or simply 'overt', of course, is a wrong act within Scientology. (Straus 1986)

This belief refers, really, to the idea that all illness is psychosomatic. It is simultaneously a holdover from the concept of providence, in which God blesses the good with good health, and a fact with which Doctors deal often when looking at the ways in which illness interacts with stress, stress being widely known to make existing issues worse, or bring them to the surface. Symptoms of unease will find their way out, and the way in which these manifest can be manifold. Of course, all illnesses are not psychosomatic as far as the evidence is concerned, but psychosomatic illnesses are real, and they are treated by medical doctors as well as psychiatrists, depending upon the particular situation. Despite their arising from the mind, they cause harm to those who experience them.

Culture bound syndromes occur when one cultural grouping recognizes a diagnosis of a medical problem-- a specific problem that does not appear in the literature in other countries or cultures. Such a diagnosis might be very old, and long accepted, or it might also be new. This problem will be diagnosed at home, where it is accepted, but outside of the bounds of that particular medical system, the expression of this illness corresponds with nothing, and it is not recognized, even if the same cluster of symptoms might be studied as an anomaly. Migration being as common as it is, we see cases of culture bound syndromes expressing themselves out of context, regardless of the fact that the constellation of symptoms and their presentation will not be received properly or given support. Many culture bound syndromes are considered by western medicine to be simply psychological complexes, a sort of *folie en masse*.

A few examples follow, before we get to our main case study. Notice that all of these illnesses primarily consist of agreed upon physical symptoms, consistent within their milieu. Heart distress is a common syndrome in Iran, appearing as shaking, fluttering, and pounding of the heart, including irregular beats, and associated with strong feelings of anxiety or anger. It often appears, seemingly in response to serious issues in the personal life of the women who identify as having it. It is considered to be a popular or folk illness, but the women who have it communicate a lot to the doctor, just by stating that they have it. (Good 1977). Heart distress says, "I'm emotionally taxed, there are changes happening in my life, and I'm having unpleasant physical symptoms." Good describes it as, "an image which draws together a network of symbols, situations, motives, feelings and stresses that are rooted in the structural setting." (1977)

Susto, also known as espanto, is an affliction widespread in Latin America. The souls of those suffering from it have wandered off, away from the physical body. There are varying beliefs as to why the soul has left, some that suggest it left willingly and others that it was stolen. Susto often follows a troubling incident in a person's life. It causes restless sleep and listless days. (Rubel 1977) Without correspondent belief in the soul as so conceived, susto cannot be recognized.

Here is a contemporary example to serve as a small case study for this chapter. We have seen stress resulting from migration and uncertainty emerging in refugees having temporary asylum within the country of Sweden. This case is interesting because this syndrome is a new development, with a new diagnostic term coming into being in 2014 after observation of similar cases since the 1990s. The Resignation syndrome, sometimes called Apathetic Syndrome, "affects mostly children, who first exhibit symptoms of depression and then withdraw from others. Eventually they stop walking, eating and talking, and grow incontinent. In the worst cases, they slip into a state of seeming unconsciousness and fail to respond to pain or other stimuli. In Sweden hundreds of migrant children, facing the possibility of deportation, have been diagnosed since the 1990s with what is known locally as resignation syndrome." (The Economist, 2018)

We can see the interaction between a set of beliefs in Sweden, and a psychological response to trauma that is guided by those beliefs, even though the children experiencing symptoms were not originally part of Swedish culture. Swedes who became involved in diagnosis and treatment began to view the syndrome as the fault of the government, who were traumatizing the children by providing them asylum and then removing or threatening to remove it. A variety of child psychologists and doctors became involved in speaking out against the policies, seeing this response as the 'cure', after witnessing that change in family residency circumstances for the better might cause the syndrome to resolve itself. Meanwhile, other children whose residency situation remained affected for years, far beyond what could be expected via an informal network of advice around deportation such as, "playing dead can delay your family's deportation, pass it on." Children were fed through tubes and unresponsive to pain, and the Swedish medical field responded by adding the diagnostic category, indicating the syndrome as an acceptable outlet of expression for unease/sickness. (Aviv 2017)

This official acceptance may have helped Swedish society to sympathize and to see the response of the children to their trauma as valid. "A hundred and sixty thousand Swedes signed a petition to stop the deportations of apathetic children and other asylum seekers. Five of Sweden's seven political parties demanded amnesty for apathetic patients…The Swedish Parliament passed a temporary act that gave thirty thousand people whose deportations were pending the right to have the Migration Board review their applications again. The board began allowing apathetic children and their families to stay." (Aviv 2017)

In other words, here we can see plainly the way that group beliefs affect sickness and health, and draw the medical field into recognizing abstract societal problems as both the cause and the solution to a serious health crisis among young refugee children. The young children were not able to consciously decide to intervene in a political process. Rather, it was the expression of their own helplessness through bodily symptoms that caused the establishment to notice the spectre of the children's disappearance.

Their weight loss and lack of response was , in a sense, a physical shutting down of vital functions, but it seems also likely to have been connected to an emotional effect that made it impossible for the children to consciously transcend, or to perceive, the illness as psychosomatic. "Western medicine focuses increasingly on the *individual* patient (or even on an individual organ), but it may be the family-- or even the community, or the wider society-- who are the pathological ones, and not the individual. An inappropriate focus only on the individual and his or her symptoms, while ignoring wider familial, social, and economic issues, may make both a consensus and a solution to the problem difficult to achieve." (Helman 1997) In Sweden's case, we see the best possible response to the syndrome came through the diagnosis and treatment of social conditions, as the medical community involved themselves in the issue and promoted asylum as the means to spare their patients.

Here, Aviv interviews one of the afflicted children for the New York Times, Geordi, from Russia. "During his months in bed, he said, he had felt as if he were in a glass box with fragile walls, deep in the ocean. If he spoke or moved, he thought, it would create a vibration, which would cause the glass to shatter. 'The water would pour in and kill me,' he said. When we had finished eating, I asked Georgi if he realized that his family had been granted residency because of him. Earnest and respectful, he considered the question as if it had been posed by a teacher. 'When I am thinking about it now, I don't think that I wanted to do this,' he told me. 'Not if I start to think about how I felt in the glass cage.'" (2017)

Swedish society, refugee families, and the medical establishment in Sweden share the belief that this type of comatose expression has a basis, a distinct etiology, and a cure. They use the same name to refer to it, so that they can collectively deal with the pain of it. This recognition causes the syndrome to remain in play, where otherwise it would be dismissed. These emotional responses and shared beliefs indicate a willingness in Sweden to adapt to situational factors resulting from the complex process of taking in refugees. The refugees, not 'seen' adequately by the legal system, which rejects their appeals, have found refuge in the medical system, and the legitimacy it confers upon them and their feelings.

I have highlighted this case because I believe, especially at this time, that cultural notions embedded within medicine need to be examined further if we are going to avoid a colonial mindset. Birth care in the United States, for instance, is failing Black women at an alarming rate-- their mortality rate when pregnant is terrifyingly high. Diagnostic tools in North America are geared to white skin. Stereotypes around which cultures are most likely to be resistant to pain, or to abuse any pills they are given, result in the pain of patients being ignored. To cure should not be to perpetuate discriminatory ideas onto those in your care. The stress of racism is lowering the life expectancy of Black people on this continent. (Saad 2020) Our beliefs find their way into the 'objective' professions. We need to identify them there, and the effects they have wrought, before they can be dealt with at all.

As you can see from the Swedish case study, shared belief isn't always a bad thing. Beliefs develop in order to account for new situations, to meet in understanding, and to reveal necessary changes that need to be made ethically. The choice to trust and to speak for the refugee children through the designation of Resignation Syndrome as a problem with a name that could be discussed and solved was an act wherein faith was placed in the children, as beings worth attending to.

Outro

A belief is more than an observation. It is a subscription, a willingness, and a cosmological location for the self. Belief is required when approaching those areas where other types of knowledge do not prove reliable, or possible: the unknown. It is an election, a choice, and with it comes certainty that would not be suitable elsewhere. Investigation does not require belief-- only supposition. Belief can reveal a hypothesis by its presence, creating a link between the known and the unknown that proves fortuitous. However, it is just as likely to hide that which is plain from view.

This book would not be useful if it did not cause you to inquire into your own beliefs, where or who they come from, and who they benefit. These questions can affect what you see as innately true, because they reveal motivations around strong beliefs, which can be heady and intoxicating when out of context. Often, beliefs settle on us and we feel them to be innate after spending a long time with them, as if they were born out of our own bodies. Many of our beliefs come out of trauma and violence, indelible in their lasting effects. There is no way to hold a completely private belief, in the sense of your belief not affecting others. Beliefs are revealed unconsciously through action.

Joining a belief system, whether it is ordered or diffuse, is generally unavoidable for functioning. Beliefs give our lives meaning and cohesion, and they direct us as we proceed through the field of interactions into which we were born. It is important to act as part of an open system, using your senses to continue to re-evaluate the situations and relations that you are part of, as they unfold. You are a being in being, as in Heidegger, and you and the web of beings that compose your environment are both constantly shifting. Remember that you have other tools of understanding beyond your own eyes, and be open to the findings of others even if they do not line up with your current beliefs. Often the fear of changing our minds prevents us from engaging outside of our belief groups. Be open to surprises, and look deeper into blind spots. Use your feelings to let you know what you need and what you envision for yourself and for others, and use evidence-based analysis to tell you whether or not those things you believe in are able to bring what you need into your sphere, as well as what the cost is to others.

Carl Jung said that, "every period has its bias, its particular prejudice, and its psychic ailment. An epoch is like an individual; it has its own limitations of conscious outlook, and therefore requires a compensatory adjustment. This is effected by the collective unconscious in that a poet, a seer or a leader allows himself to be guided by the unexpressed desire of his times and shows the way, by word or deed, to the attainment of that which everyone blindly craves and expects-- whether this attainment results in good or evil, the healing of an epoch or its destruction." (1933)

In my opinion, the refusal by many to engage with ethical issues is a sad gift from capitalism and Cartesian dualism, separating us into bodies, which want what they want, and souls, who can contemplate goodness in the abstract. It may also be related to a philosophical issue dating back all the way to Ancient Greece, and touched upon by thinkers like Arendt and Foucault. "Plato was the first to introduce the division between those who know and do not act and those who act and do not know, instead of the old articulation of action into beginning and achieving, so that knowing what to do and doing it became two altogether different performances." (Arendt 1958)

I want to end by examining an article on divinatory practices that I found buried in an anthropological compilation on the theme of the relationship between the environment and culture. The article examines the functions of local beliefs in divination among the Naskapi in Quebec and Northern Labrador, and it is called Divination-- A New Perspective, by Omar Khayyan Moore (1969). I want to be clear that the name Naskapi is not what this indigenous group calls themselves, and that I am not sure whether this practice continues to be part of their present day culture in 2020. The proper name for the group is Innu. I want to use this article in an illustrative capacity, but for current information, you should use another source.

Moore starts by explaining that magical practices, though useful when serving as social rituals to bond the group, have classically been considered inefficacious toward the actual problem that they are intended to solve. Moore says that, "Magic is, by definition and reputation, a notoriously ineffective method for attaining the specific ends its practitioners hope to achieve through its use...Most, if not all, scientific analyses of magic presuppose that these rituals as a matter of fact do not lead to the desired results...One of the puzzles most theorists of magic seeks to resolve is why human beings cling so tenaciously to magic if it does not work." (1969)

However, in the course of studying Innu divination, Moore came up with a thesis that surprised him. He found a useful function was brought into operation by the choice to base hunting decisions upon the markings on a reindeer bone. That function was the introduction of randomness into the situation, and the purpose that it served was to direct hunting in cases when the group was already out of known options. When they know a plentiful place to hunt, the Naskapi (Innu) do not use the method. Moore tells us that, "In the divinatory ritual the shoulder blade, thus prepared, is held over hot coals for a short time. The heat causes cracks and burnt spots to form, and these are then 'read.'...One class of questions for which shoulder-blade augury provides answers is: What direction should hunters take in locating game? This is a critical matter, for the failure of a hunt may bring privation or even death."

Moore goes on to describe the way in which the bone serves as a map of the geographic area for the hunting ground, with splits in the bone after the fire indicating paths in one direction or another. By bringing in an interaction with forces outside of themselves, the Innu let go of control, and yielded the choice of where to hunt to chance, or to fate if you prefer. But why was this advantageous, and what have they gained by incorporating this belief, and its attendant randomness?

Moore indicates that, based on his observations, "there may be a marked advantage in avoiding a fixed pattern in hunting. Unwitting regularities in behaviour provide a basis for anticipatory responses...it would seem that a certain amount of irregularity would be introduced to the Naskapi (Innu) hunting pattern by this mechanism...In the first place, the Naskapi (Innu)live a precarious life; their continued existence depends on the success of their day-to-day hunting. And it is prima facie unlikely that grossly defective approaches to hunting would have survival value...Under these circumstances, a device which would break up habit patterns in a more or less random fashion might be of value."

Moore goes on to explain why one might need the device of belief in divination in order to access randomness. Randomness is not something that we can easily or consciously generate, in and of ourselves. Attempting to generate randomness knowingly is futile because its nature is to be pattern-less and we are patterning and associative, as individuals and in our groups. So the Innu, in Moore's opinion, had created a useful concept for themselves by recognizing that their own hunting choice patterning was having an effect on the animals of the area, who were basically learning to avoid them. By seeking an answer from another source, they were able to change their hunting patterns in order to remain ahead of the curve.

Evidently, group beliefs of the best kind open us up. They expand us. They are useful to us by providing avenues towards the ideals that we seek, whatever those may be. They also, unavoidably, plug us into systems of power creating ills and benefits that we must be ever aware of.

Sources

intro:

Arendt, Hannah 1958 The Human Condition. University of Chicago Press

James, William, 1900 On A Certain Blindness in Human Beings & Varieties of the Religious Experience 1902

Jung, Karl 1933 Modern Man In Search of a Soul Published: Kegan Paul, Trench, Trubner and Co, London

Kidder Model Of Decision Making in Media Ethics, Journal of Mass Media Ethics, Vol. 12, No. 4, 1997, p.205

Sweet, Louise E. Camel Pastoralism in North Arabia and the Minimal Camping Unit, from Vayda, Andrew P (editor) 1969 Environment and Cultural Behaviour

Mormon section:

https://www.quora.com/Is-the-Book-Of-Mormon-historically-accurate

Benjamin, Perry Pierce. The Origin of the "Book of Mormon" Source: American Anthropologist , Oct., 1899, New Series, Vol. 1, No. 4 (Oct., 1899), pp.675-694 Published by: Wiley on behalf of the American Anthropological Association Stable URL: http://www.jstor.com/stable/658645

Clark, John E. Archaeological Trends and Book of Mormon Origins Source: Brigham Young University Studies , 2005, Vol. 44, No. 4, The Worlds of Joseph Smith: A BICENTENNIAL CONFERENCE AT THE LIBRARY OF CONGRESS (2005), pp. 83-104 Published by: Brigham Young University Stable URL: http://www.jstor.com/stable/43045053

Frey, S. (1879). Were they Mound-Builders? The American Naturalist, 13(10), 637-644. Retrieved August 25, 2020, from http://www.jstor.org/stable/2449295

King, David S. "Proving" the Book of Mormon: Archaeology Vs. Faith. Source: Dialogue: A Journal of Mormon Thought , Spring 1991, Vol. 24, No. 1 (Spring 1991), pp. 143-146 Published by: University of Illinois Press Stable URL: http://www.jstor.com/stable/45227736

Laruelle, Marlene, Conspiracy and Alternate History in Russia: A Nationalist Equation for Success? Source: The Russian Review, Vol. 71, No. 4 (OCTOBER 2012), pp. 565-580 Published by: Wiley on behalf of The Editors and Board of Trustees of the Russian Review

Metcalfe, Brent Lee. Apologetic and Critical Assumptions about Book of Mormon Historicity. Source: Dialogue: A Journal of Mormon Thought , Fall 1993, Vol. 26, No. 3 (Fall 1993), pp. 153-184. Published by: University of Illinois Press Stable URL: http://www.jstor.com/stable/45228673

Mueller, Max Perry Chapter Title: THE BOOK OF MORMON: A (White) Universal Gospel . Book Title: Race and the Making of the Mormon People Published by: University of North Carolina Press. Stable URL: http://www.jstor.com/stable/10.5149/9781469633763_mueller.6

Price, Robert M. Joseph Smith in the Book of Mormon Source: Dialogue: A Journal of Mormon Thought , Winter 2003, Vol. 36, No. 4 (Winter 2003), pp. 89-96

Published by: University of Illinois Press. Stable URL: http://www.jstor.com/stable/45227187

Smith, Alana . Messianic Time and The Book of Mormon Source: Journal of Book of Mormon Studies , Vol. 27 (2018), pp. 197-209 Published by: University of Illinois Press. Stable URL: https://www.jstor.org/stable/10.5406/jbookmormstud2.27.2018.0197

Bosnia section:

Youtube Videos cited, and central site:

http://piramidasunca.ba/bs/ - main website for the Archaeological Park

https://www.youtube.com/watch?v=pwTuw5BPqU0 - Youtube user Travis Bryant proves by looking

https://www.youtube.com/watch?v=T7j_jzWYJQA - woman leads you through Ravne tunnels by user AV Daniel Violin

https://www.youtube.com/watch?v=OeeSwNcMGv0 - healing energy claims

https://www.youtube.com/watch?v=GvJ_mKogBKM - rocks set to soaring music by user Picture Choice TV with the label, "the history of humanity must be rewritten"

https://www.youtube.com/watch?v=lUut8XePF-Y - Semir tours the Pyramid of the Sun

https://www.youtube.com/watch?v=NNxNKIbPuHM - ions touted as a solution for viruses by Semir

https://www.youtube.com/watch?v=CKxmkjsf4mk - video by SBResearch Group investigating infrasounds at the complex

https://www.youtube.com/watch?v=TCzz1ymta5s - volunteers excavating from all around the world are interviewed

https://www.youtube.com/watch?v=JTHPtF2Nd74 - 'all as one' : volunteer excavation

https://www.youtube.com/watch?v=0sEKQkZOcGc&feature=youtu.be - Dr. Semir - My Story

Articles:

Archived statement by European Archaeologists:

https://web.archive.org/web/20110717134402/http://www.e-a-a.org/statement.pdf

Edelman, Murray 1985 The Symbolic Uses of Politics, paperback ed, University of Illinois press

Harding, Anthony (January–February 2007). Pitts, Mike (ed.). "The great Bosnian pyramid scheme". British Archaeology. No. 92. Council for British Archaeology

Harris, Lucian "Amateur to dig on site of medieval capital in search of Bosnia's own Valley of the Kings", *The Art Newspaper*, 15 April 2006

Heinrich, Paul V . Pseudoscience in Bosnia Source: Science, New Series, Vol. 318, No. 5847 (Oct. 5, 2007), pp. 42-43 Published by: American Association for the Advancement of Science

Ramadanovic, Jusuf (18 September 2008). "Archaeologists find medieval artefacts on Mt. Visocica, disparage pyramid seeker". Southeast European Times.

Traynor, Ian (5 October 2006). "Tourists flock to Bosnian hills but experts mock amateur archaeologist's pyramid claims". The Guardian.

Freemen On the Land/Strawman section:

https://www.embassyofheaven.com/ - Paul Revere's blog

https://www.adl.org/resources/backgrounders/sovereign-citizen-movement – Anti Defamation League statement

https://www.canlii.org/en/ab/abqb/doc/2012/2012abqb571/2012abqb571.html - Mead court case summary

McDowall, Robert. The Folklore of Finance Source: Folklore , December 2013, Vol. 124, No. 3 (December 2013), pp. 253-264 Published by: Taylor & Francis, Ltd. on behalf of Folklore Enterprises, Ltd.

McRoberts, Colin editor Powell, Corey (March 21, 2016). "Here comes pseudolaw, a weird little cousin of pseudoscience". Aeon.

Monat section:

The Dream Podcast – Stitcher find via your podcast app or at https://www.stitcher.com/podcast/stitcher/the-dream

Moreno et al. Cyberpsychol Behav Soc Netw. 2013 Sep; 16(9): 708–713.doi: 10.1089/cyber.2012.0334PMCID: PMC3942703 PMID: 23679571 Ethics of Social Media Research: Common Concerns and Practical Considerations Megan A. Moreno, MD, MSEd, MPH, corresponding author1 Natalie Goniu,1 Peter S. Moreno, MS, JD,2 and Douglas Diekema, MD, MPH access: https://www.ncbi.nlm.nih.gov/pmc/articles/PMC3942703/

Schieman, Scott & Jung, Jong Hyun "Practical Divine Influence": Socioeconomic Status and Belief in the Prosperity Gospel Source: Journal for the Scientific Study of Religion , DECEMBER 2012, Vol. 51, No. 4 (DECEMBER 2012), pp. 738-756 Published by: Wiley on behalf of Society for the Scientific Study of Religion

Vesoulis, Abby and Dockterman, Eliana . Pandemic Schemes. Time Magazine, August 2020

Shared Delusions: Courts section

https://theoutline.com/post/2066/most-criminal-cases-end-in-plea-bargains-not-trials

Cialdini, Robert 1985 Influence: Science and Practice, 5th Edition | Pearson

Donoghue, Joan E . The Effectiveness of the International Court of Justice Source: Proceedings of the Annual Meeting (American Society of International Law) , Vol. 108, The Effectiveness of International Law (2014), pp. 114-118 Published by: Cambridge University Press on behalf of the American Society of International Law Stable URL:
https://www.jstor.org/stable/10.5305/procannmeetasil.108.0114

Falk, Sally Moore. 1969 Selection For Failure In a Small Social Field in Symbolism and Communal Ideology 1975 Cornell University Press

International Court of Justice Source: The International and Comparative Law Quarterly, Vol. 20, No. 2 (Apr., 1971), pp. 354-357 Published by: Cambridge University Press on behalf of the British Institute of International and Comparative Law Stable URL:
https://www.jstor.org/stable/758040

Paulson, Colter Compliance with Final Judgments of the International Court of Justice since 1987Source: The American Journal of International Law , Jul., 2004, Vol. 98, No. 3 (Jul.,2004), pp. 434-461 Published by: Cambridge University Press Stable URL:
http://www.jstor.com/stable/3181640

Posner, Eric A & de Figueiredo, Miguel F.P. Is the International Court of Justice Biased? Source: The Journal of Legal Studies , Vol. 34, No. 2 (June 2005), pp. 599-630 Published by: The

University of Chicago Press for The University of Chicago Law School . Stable URL:

https://www.jstor.org/stable/10.1086/430765

Powell, Emilia Justyna Islamic law states and the International Court of Justice Source: Journal of Peace Research, Vol. 50, No. 2 (March 2013), pp. 203-217 Published by: Sage Publications, Ltd. Stable URL: https://www.jstor.org/stable/23441186

Shapiro, Martin 1986 Courts: A Comparative and Political Analysis . The University of Chicago Press (paperback edition)

Tibbetts, Stephen 2018 ed. Criminological Theory: The Essentials SAGE Publications

Culture-Bound Syndromes section

Aviv, Rachel. The Trauma of Facing Deportation March 2017 The New Yorker

https://www.newyorker.com/magazine/2017/04/03/the-trauma-of-facing-deportation

Bainbridge, William Sims & Stark, Rodney. Scientology: To Be Perfectly Clear Source: Sociological Analysis, Vol. 41, No. 2 (Summer, 1980), pp. 128-136 Published by: Oxford University Press Stable URL: https://www.jstor.org/stable/3709904

Good, B 1977 The heart of what's the matter: the semantics of illness in Iran. Cult. Med. Psychiatry

Helman, Cecil G. 1997 ed. Culture, Health and Illness 3rd Edition

Klein, Norman (ed.). 1979 Culture, Curers & Contagion. Chandler & Sharp

Rubel, A.J 1977 The epidemiology of a folk illness: Susto in Hispanic America in Landy, D ed. Culture, Disease and Healing New York:Macmillan

Saad, Layla Me and White Supremacy Jan 2020

Shipler, David K . More Schoolgirls in West Bank Fall Sick April 4th 1983

https://www.nytimes.com/1983/04/04/world/more-schoolgirls-in-west-bank-fall-sick.html

Straus, Roger Scientology "Ethics": Deviance, Identity and Social Control in a Cult-Like Social World Source: Symbolic Interaction , Vol. 9, No. 1 (Spring 1986), pp. 67-82 Published by: Wiley on behalf of the Society for the Study of Symbolic Interaction Stable URL:

https://www.jstor.org/stable/10.1525/si.1986.9.1.67

"U.S. Experts Blame Anxiety For Illness of West Bank Girls", The New York Times, April 25, 1983

Von Folsach, Liv Lyngå; Montgomery, Edith (July 2006). "Pervasive refusal syndrome among asylum-seeking children". Clinical Child Psychology and Psychiatry. 11 (3): 457–473. doi:10.1177/1359104506064988. ISSN 1359-1045. PMID 17080781

What Is Resignation Syndrome. The Economist

https://www.economist.com/the-economist-explains/2018/10/24/what-is-resignation-syndrome

Outro

Arendt, Hannah 1958 The Human Condition. University of Chicago Press

Karl Jung, Modern Man in Search of a Soul 1933 Published: Kegan Paul, Trench, Trubner and Co, London

Moore, Omar Khayyan Divination-- A New Perspective, in Environment and Cultural Behaviour ed Andrew P. Vayda. American Museum Sourcebooks in Anthropology 1969

www.ingramcontent.com/pod-product-compliance
Lightning Source LLC
Chambersburg PA
CBHW051213250726

48655CB00006B/2381